DEAR MOTHER

LETTERS FROM THE HEART

Suma Din

KUBE

Dear Mother: Letters from the Heart

First published in England by
Kube Publishing Ltd, Markfield Conference Centre,
Ratby Lane Markfield, Leicestershire LE67 9SY, United Kingdom.

Distributed by
Kube Publishing Ltd.
Tel: +44(0)1530 249230 email: info@kubepublishing.com

A special thank you to Deqa Mohamed for allowing us
to use her poem *Dhexda xirol – tie your waist* in the book.

Cataloguing-in-Publication Data is available from the British library

ISBN 978-1-84774-203-2 Hardback
ISBN 978-1-84774-204-9 ebook

Cover design and internal typesetting: Nasir Cadir
Cover wreath and motif design: Iman Anwar
Printed in: Turkey by Elma Basim

CONTENTS

DEDICATION

Dedicated to the memory of my grandmothers
Mehrunessa Ghaffur & *Firoza Begum*

Whose labour in raising their families
bore fruits across many generations.
May they be rewarded with eternal
serenity in the gardens of *Jannat al-Firdaws*.

Āmīn.

ACKNOWLEDGEMENTS

All thanks and praise are first to Allah ﷻ for the opportunity and resources to pour time and effort into this book. Any good that comes from this work is through His permission. I seek His forgiveness for any mistakes in it, which are solely mine.

Books, like babies, come with their own provision, and I've felt this more tangibly with this book. This provision has come in the form of enlightening people of all ages: students, colleagues, friends, family and virtual acquaintances. There are far too many people I would like to thank than I have space for here. I'm truly grateful to everyone I've discussed motherhood with; women and men who do not have children, as well as those who are parents.

In particular, I'm grateful to these generous women who provided written critical feedback on specific letters. They are: Sadiya Ahmed, Mariam Akhtar, Anisa Ather, Adiba Borsha, Saleema Burney, Sarah Gulamhusein, Mariam

K S Hakim, Haaniah Hamid, Neila Hayat, Nazli Hussain, Elizabeth Lymer and Eman Nabi. Thank you to Khadijah Hayley for her valuable comments at an early stage of writing this book.

For helping with research queries, thank you to Zirrar Ali, Fouzia Dualeh, Amina Dahir, Safura Houghton, Monira Khanom, Saira Qureshi, and the founder of the Muslim Mamas, Nargis Jahan-Uddin, for the access she gave me to the wonderful mothers from the Muslim Mamas Angels group. Thank you to every mother who wrote back to me from this group. For the kind permission to use her poem, *Tie Your Waist!* thank you to poet and writer, Deqa Mohamed.

I'm indebted to all at Kube Publishing for working on this book. Thank you to the Director, Haris Ahmad, for taking this title on, and to Kube's team behind the scenes who look after all the steps of production. Very special appreciation to the editor of this book Dr Lubaaba Al-Azami for her many insights on the subject matter as well as her rigour and attention to detail. It has been a pleasure and honour to work with her.

I thank my mother for her direct input, helping me with aspects of Bangla vocabulary and culture. I thank her also for supporting hours upon hours of my 'present absence', sitting near her working away on this manuscript. I'm grateful to my husband, Asad, for weathering the doubts and storms that accompanied writing this book. It wasn't easy and I thank you for the constant patience as well as the space and time to get on with it.

Finally thank you to our three children, Haaniah, Nabihah and Ibrahim, for your input which has been practical, critical, patient and supportive in the right doses at the right times! Unlike other books, I could only write this one because you were all on board with its purpose and intention.

INTRODUCTION

Dear Reader,

In a book of fictional letters, the introduction has to be a letter and it has to be a real one to you. We don't know each other but we have one thing in common: we started life in our mothers' wombs. What happened to both of us after our births may be very different but our shared beginning is enough of a connection between us.

It's this universal connection that makes the subject of motherhood so emotive. Unlike any other relationship, this 'tie of the womb' gives birth to an array of deeply held feelings based on our own experiences. As much as childhood is a time of innocence, growth, awe and wonder, nurturing a child isn't a parallel experience. Motherhood is a magnificent, humbling, chaotic experience; physically, emotionally, mentally and spiritually. It's an ongoing, invisible labour of love, long after the umbilical cord is cut.

Given the strong views held, why would I or anyone else write about the maternal journey? I've questioned myself about this scores of times. The answer lies at the source of most endeavours, if we dig deep enough: it's personal. So, here's a window into my mothering experience and the motivation for writing this book.

When the clear blue line appeared in the plastic rectangular window less than two centimetres in length, it signposted my life in a new direction: pregnancy and motherhood. I pushed fears about childbirth to the back of my mind and willingly embraced pregnancy, convinced by the fact that millions of women giving birth around the globe must mean it's easy and natural. And I had the same thoughts about raising children; how hard could it be, everyone does it? I was fortunate to have an extended family around me on a regular basis, so I saw babies joining the family and toddlers growing up into intriguing characters. I enjoyed seeing their personalities grow. It looked easy enough. From there I set off for a walk down an imaginary motherhood lane, lined with wildflowers and hanging boughs of roses, beyond which lay a vista of maternal fulfilment...

I was twenty-three years old, expecting our first child. I swelled with naivety before the signs of any pregnancy showed. Having got married while still at university, I had spent the previous two years in undergraduate and then postgraduate studies without any real plan about what I'd do in my field of education apart from teaching. Becoming a mother was welcomed wholeheartedly as a blessing and, at that point in my life, a marker of moving on from student life to parenthood. Maybe the context of our birth isn't something we think about much, but it matters.

If you're a mother reading this, your path may well have been very different to mine, experiencing pregnancy at a different stage of life, or becoming a parent through adoption, or as a step-mum. Or perhaps you're a mother figure in a child's life, alongside their parents. Each way has its own learning curve.

I look back now, over a quarter of a century later, with the benefit of hindsight. I see the blessings that came with our three children. I see the growth we underwent as parents alongside them. I see the chasm between what I thought the maternal journey was going to be and the reality.

Some of my expectations did materialise. I found ample contentment and joy in the baby stage and early years in particular. Even when our third child introduced us to what real sleep deprivation meant, month on month, year on year, there was still a deep feeling of gratitude for and pleasure with our growing family, albeit through dazed and foggy brains. In those days, local mothers and I were busy creating informal toddler groups. We coordinated with health visitors to run parenting courses for us. We created art or story sessions around Eid and Ramadan and simply came together socially as our babies grew up in front of us.

As the journey continued, parenting got more complex, as you would recognise if you have reached that stage. The enormity of the responsibility grew and the pressures on this role, especially from external factors, meant there were plenty of challenges. Figuring out whether or not they celebrated birthdays, like the rest of the children in their class, was a minor issue compared to the effects of peer pressure or finding suitable TV programmes for them. These issues then became of less importance when bigger hurdles came our way. Going through distressing life events, like the death of a class friend in primary school or the passing away of a grandparent, were things we parents were never fully prepared for. Our children learnt how fragile life was, and we learnt how to keep a sense of balance for them through these experiences.

Secondary school years are renowned for a never-ending list of challenges: the nightmare of smart phones in our children's lives, for example, and the introduction of iPads in the education system which intruded on whatever was left of their web free childhood. All the choices and decisions that were on their shoulders at a young age were dealt with differently by each child. And as parents, we had to find what worked and what didn't, seeing our children as individuals. The securitization issues out in the public domain, became part of mum talk too. Whatever age our children were, I found myself engaged in many conversations, often listening incredulously to another mother's account of an incident experienced by her family. This wasn't exactly the motherhood landscape I expected.

Universal parental angst was alive and well as some readers would recognise either from being on the receiving end, or as uneasy parents. What did constitute too much support, what did constitute too little? How far was being part of the crowd going to help the children and when would it hinder them? How do you keep extended family relationships alive in a society which relentlessly teaches the 'me, myself and I' mantra? How do you manage your own development as a person, as a Muslim, as a mother, and as a role model under the microscope of three pairs of eyes, twenty-four hours a day, seven days a week?

Browsing parenting books or blogs and talking to friends is something we are all likely to have done along the way. I listened to elders' observations, bonded with mothers who were complete strangers, cried and laughed, finished and started, several times over – seeking one thing: to understand 'mother work' in today's context. The books I reached for in the early days were on practical mechanics; from potty-training to sibling rivalry and beyond. Later on, I reached for books written by mothers exploring their personal journeys, which resonated with me but only partly. While there were compelling discussions about topics such as a mother's work-life balance, in these writings, they didn't include other parts of the equation that mattered to me, such as caring for ageing parents, accountability in the Hereafter and spending time and effort to help one's children get married.

None of the writers seemed to understand the particular type of mothering I, and, as I later realised, hundreds of thousands of us were doing. The type of mothering that comes from being a second-generation child of immigrant parents in a country that has a different heritage and paradigm to your family's background. A type of mothering where you must construct your parenting framework day by day – even though you have parents' and elders' examples in front of you. It's a type of mothering in which faith is the foundation, and you have to find the pieces to complete the structure. A type of mothering in which the environment changes all of a sudden. How do you navigate it, unprepared? A type of mothering where you don't need more instructions and rules, but more understanding and empathy.

Empathy was what I was looking for then, as a new and young mother. And this need remains the same even now. There's something comforting about sharing one's journey, which is as natural as sharing a spectacular view with a companion or reaching out to a friend when in fear. Women are good at sharing, but so often those few words of empathy and understanding aren't there when they're needed the most.

This collection of fictional letters comes partly from the dialogues I've had all these years with women from around the globe who happened to be a part of my life, whether for a few minutes or several years. Some were mothers and some were not, but together our interactions helped me look at this role through many different eyes.

The letters here explore issues close to our hearts, attempting to capture the daily pulse of a variety of mothers' lives; those moments that seem to last for an eternity, those parenting quandaries that land in our laps unannounced. The snapshots of maternal life covered here are limited, and I don't pretend to cover the endless variety of situations that mothers find themselves in. I wrestled with the dilemma of not covering many issues close to my heart; infertility, the loss of a child, the challenges of various educational systems, being a mother-in-law, being a foster mother, amongst many more. Hence, this collection is a start and just that.

A young, self-assured optician once decided to be cordial during a routine eye-test. He asked me what I do. I replied at the time I was in the midst of interviewing mothers for some research. He asked what the research was about. I told him the title of the book it was intended for.[1]

'Why have you got 'Muslim Mothers' in the title, why not just mothers? Keep your left eye on that light, please.'

'Why not? This is how the mothers identify themselves. They've got different demands on them... their experiences include their faith.' And in case that wasn't enough, I continued 'So why would I leave out a big part of who they are?'

'How's your vision when you're driving? Most people are struggling at your age, varifocals might be an option.'

Cordiality box ticked, the examination continued in silence.

Amir, or Ahmed, perhaps it was Ali, his name faded in my memory over time. But his critique reinforced the need to make space – several more spaces – for our faith-centred framework to be prioritised. I wondered if this young man, obviously from a South Asian background, ever considered the work of his mother, or whoever raised him, as any different from what *all* mothers do? Perhaps his mother/ guardian's work blended into the commonplace fixtures of their home; like a door, a window, the kettle in the kitchen. Maybe the mother/guardian's struggles weren't discussed openly. Perhaps he would rather not think about mothers at

---

1   *Muslim Mothers and their Children's Schooling* (2017), Trentham Press.

all for a good reason, I'll never know. But it got me thinking from yet another perspective: does the faith-centric journey of mothers matter to the new generation, or to anyone else? Thanks to that young optician I got more out of the sight-test than I anticipated.

A few words about fathers and all others who play a significant part in the parenting journey. Although the collection is specifically speaking to mothers, it's not intended to devalue the fathers' contribution, or anyone else's efforts to raise children. The struggles fathers face deserves a space of their own. If you're a son, father or both reading this, I hope you gain something from it too.

Foresight, hindsight, perspective or blind spot, the way we look at motherhood changes from one place to another and from one mother to another. It's vital that we see this role from as many angles as possible, and that it is felt in all its variance. You will, no doubt, bring your own narrative to these pages too and I hope it leads to much discussion.

I am grateful to have your time, engaging with the subject of motherhood. This is one way of pushing it up on our collective agenda where it deserves to be. It's up to us to reclaim the space that honours a mother's spiritual and emotional labours amongst all the other forms of her effort. This is our space.

With love and hope,
Suma

'I am *al-Raḥmān*.
I created the *Raḥim* (womb)
and derived a name for it from My Name.

Hence whoever keeps it (family ties), I will keep ties with
him, and whoever severs it, I will sever ties with him.'
Ḥadīth Qudsī

1

DEAR MOTHER
WHO HAS A SECOND JOB

From:

Dina, A 'working' mother

Home Number 1 – infinity

Every street, lane, road, drive or close

Every village, town, city, district

Every country

Since the beginning of time

Salaams,

How are you doing Salma?

Surprised to receive a letter from me? I felt the urge and grabbed that letter writing set that's been sat in the drawer for a year. And so here you go – a letter about things I wanted to capture before the thoughts are lost, like the elusive odd socks that break free from the washing machine.

Last week, during our video call – our lifeline in this pandemic – you said, casually, 'Well I don't have a job, I'm just at home doing the kids' stuff.' Even though we carried on talking, your words kept playing back at night. I knew I had to come back to this, and come back in full! So, this is coming from my heart, head and gut, partly composed during another insomnia episode.

Every mother is working. You know that deep down inside! If raising the next generation, developing their spiritual, moral and emotional selves as well as supporting all the rest of their education isn't a 'job', or isn't 'work', then what is? Sadly, when answering the 'what do you do?'

question, there's an uncomfortable, apologetic voice in us that takes over. I know, as I'm on a war path to stop myself from saying the very same lines I heard last week.

Maybe it's the *way* we are asked the dreaded 'So what do you do?' It's such a loaded question; full of historical, cultural, social and economic shifts that have taken place, and then used as a search warrant to analyse our lives. And it's that tone – you know, *that* one. It's not once or twice I've had that question asked with a sneer, when the questioner knows I don't have a 'paid' job, but gets some pleasure reinforcing their own assumptions and bias. 'And you raised yourself?' is what I've felt like saying a few times, but of course I didn't.

It's funny how friends and relatives who live in so-called 'less developed' countries don't get asked this question. It's implicitly understood that they are raising families. Their contribution to society is so obvious, mothers don't have to spell it out. Ironically, in the more economically wealthy countries, the question rolls off people's tongues. And if we're not asked, then we, the mothers, start to apologise for our child-raising work. We are caught in that deficit mind-set that only paid work is worthy of being called 'work'.

Working as a 'mother' is an honour. When we believe it's an honour and walk like it's an honour and talk like it's an honour, then others might start looking at our role as something honourable too. Whether the role is dressed in the outfits of 'care work', 'stay at home mother (SAHM)', 'homemaker', or simply 'mother raising kids', it's a huge contribution to our family units, community and society; regardless of any labels. And if it needs to be compared to the professional world, then it would take at least five professionals to cover our job description – and that's being optimistic!

I can hear you thinking I'm being touchy and over sensitive and, I guess, I am. You know that I react to things! But on this topic, it's not a reaction as such. It's more like thoughts that have built up over the past couple of years. And you know what, Sal, it's not just personal. It's a common problem, this feeling that our work of raising children doesn't count somehow. Even though we've both got such different situations, we know what we're doing is teamwork with our husbands. It's working together that keeps the family going. Why is this division of labour not good enough? It works all over the world. Someone working outside, and someone managing the home and children, is a fluid partnership that adjusts over time.

We've just seen how it took a global pandemic for society to acknowledge what's been hidden and dealt with as though it's not happening: the work of raising children and managing the home. As long as the young ones were kept in schools and other childcare provisions, i.e. out of professional people's way, all was good. With the pandemic and lockdowns, the reality dawned that there is actually a significant 'job' going on inside the home. Finally, the world had to stop and look at what happens behind the front door and the energy and time it takes to do all these caring roles for the young and the elderly.

It feels so cathartic putting all this in a letter to you, Salma, as I've had this on my mind for quite a while. So many more questions bounce off this idea that raising a family is 'not work' – maybe that's the cause of tonight's insomnia! Questions like how do we define 'work'? And what's the measure we're using to weigh up our roles? And how did the harsh divide come about between working in and outside the home? And that big subject of why women judge one another harshly about whether they're working outside or inside the home or both, as is the reality for so many of us. We need to support one another, there's enough responsibility we're shouldering already.

Working outside the home is literally taking on a second job. To those who can, it's fantastic when it's a choice that the couple make, especially if they have the support to go with that. We've both had jobs outside, too, sometimes out of necessity, sometimes when an opportunity arose to use our skills. We understand how hard it is to make those decisions; there are so many factors at play. We know several mothers, though, who have no choice and are doing both jobs – often without enough support.

We've got other friends and relatives who prefer to blend their child-raising and working in their profession in new ways. And then there are others who've taken on voluntary roles in things they're passionate about.

You and I both worked outside, before we had children and you've done short stints in between having children too. And we know from what we've read that Muslim women have always contributed intellectually, spiritually, in business and commerce, in discoveries, in languages and legal professions, across the world. Our contribution to society isn't what's got to me right now. What has got to me is how we think about and present the work we do inside the home: where does that figure in the idea of 'contribution to society'?

But now that I've mentioned it, external jobs for us mothers are never straightforward either. Feeling guilty, burning out, taking on the double role of inside and outside responsibilities; there's a whole lot there to discuss. Listening to everyone's assumptions and opinions about why mothers are working outside: damned if you do, damned if you don't, isn't it? It's a bit easier to handle all this when going out to work is a choice. But the reality is that most women don't get to choose because of the cost of living.

Between us friends we talk about how much our faith values our role as 'family builders'. And then you only have to talk to someone – a shop assistant, your dentist or have some small talk at a bank counter – and the value system is the opposite. The 'So you don't do anything' theme is on replay again. That's what feeds some of the internal conflict: we uphold one value system while the world around us is turned on its head.

Out there, it's material productivity – GDP and economic contribution are all that a person's worth is measured by. Tax systems penalise families that have one parent stay at home to raise children. Policies have weird ways of looking for solutions through increasing childcare provision, rather than making it economically viable for mothers who want to stay at home because they believe it's best for their children. Instead of helping mothers, the system is constructed in a way that feels like it 'fines' families that have one earning parent while the other doesn't earn.

From our *dīn*, motherhood – whether that's as a foster

mother or birth mother – is honoured in the highest terms. The Sunnah is full of examples of this. The Qur'ānic message on this is clear too. Female uniqueness, abilities, wiring and contributions to society in the widest sense are there, and always have been, if we look carefully.

There's a constant dialogue going on in society about the mental, physical and emotional strain on the women who shoulder the home management job and their paid job. And single mothers, like my own mother, are warriors on the frontline. My mother struggled alone, raising the four of us, and also earning a living from home. She made sure we all got fed, clothed and benefitted from a decent education. She sacrificed her time and energy for us at every turn. There are no words to express how much I respect single mothers.

We need to create *our* own language about *our* own reality, until people learn to speak to us using *our* vocabulary: to acknowledge that every mother is working. That's the starting point of any conversation about 'what do you do?'.

I hope we mothers can support each other in our struggles to do this job the best we can. It's not easy at the best of times, and every bit of understanding helps. It's not a race or competition, is it, between who does which job? We're all paving a path into the future, and we all need to lay down pieces to help each other move ahead.

I look forward to the weekend when you'll be coming over to stay, *in shā' Allāh.*

Love and hugs,
Dina.

2

DEAR MOTHER
IN THE ANTENATAL CLINIC

From:
A mother expecting her fourth baby
At the antenatal clinic
Sitting across the waiting room
Last week

*Salām*s to you sister,

I recognise your state. You've found yourself here but you're not sure why. If someone were to ask, you'd know what to say, 'I'm here for my eight-week appointment.'

I recognise that look of displacement on you. Your gaze is fixed towards the window, head angled away from the rest of us in the waiting room. Outside the window is a brick wall.

I recognise that posture, perched on your seat on the precipice of retching because the air everyone else breaths effortlessly, smells nauseating. Inhaling is work, exhaling a relief, that familiar struggle, at times, to stay upright in public.

It's my fourth time here; royal blue antenatal folder in hand. Still carrying an oversized handbag with half the house in it and wearing a jersey maternity top from the last time around; the wardrobe's still half-full of them. What are pre-pregnancy clothes anyway, a smaller number on the tag to make us feel good?

This is your third, I'm guessing. Roughly three years after your last one, judging from the height of your youngest.

That's a nice gap. I saw your other half outside the reception with your two little boys, dropping you off. I guess he's going to keep them occupied while you get on with the appointment.

Since they left you've dropped the drained smile and your eyes are aligned with how you're feeling: uncertain. I hear that sigh in the wordless way women communicate with each other. It says that unlike the pregnancy testing adverts where the actress with flawless skin and salon styled hair exudes joy at seeing the blue line appear, you're not elated but a bit numb. It's not always instant joy and tearful smiles with a friend positioned opposite you in a designer kitchen waiting to celebrate.

Sometimes, it's mixed feelings: gratitude, surprise, confusion and fear. Fear about the timing; fear about your situation or health; fear about the pregnancy and birth; fear about how you'll fit another human being's needs into an already stretched 24 hours.

The third time I saw the blue line I had mixed feelings too. Actually, by that time, I had lost control of how I felt as I was held hostage by my hormones' mayhem. The one memory I can recall from that state of confusion was how I would cope with another little life totally dependent on me when I felt I was barely managing with the needs of the two children we already had.

At that moment in time, the fear was real, growing with the nausea, by the minute. That was what prompted the pregnancy test in the first place. I was walking through the fragrance department in Boots that morning, and out of nowhere felt the unstoppable urge to vomit right there. I lurched for the nearest exit, dropping the empty basket by the door, and breathed in deeply. The fresh air did the job and the urge to be sick subsided.

I couldn't understand why the blameless tea and toast I'd eaten two hours earlier induced a sickness like I was on a ship in a storm. That morning marked a ban on the mention and sight of 'TEA' for the next eight months. My husband couldn't believe how the third pregnancy could be so different and the nausea triggers so specific. His shower gel, his shampoo and musk had the same effect: intolerable surges of stomach-churning sickness. That feeling in the pit of my stomach told me more than any test could.

I arrived for my first antenatal appointment in the company of fear. 'Oh you'll forget the labour the moment you see the baby,' friends told me in good faith. Every detail of the two labours were neatly filed in my memory – as meticulous as the midwife's notes.

I never forgot.

Over time though, I learnt to see that fear as part of the struggle all child-bearing women might face in their own ways. Even the most noble of women felt pain and experienced fear, I realised. So even though those memories were fixed like spokes in a wheel, at the centre of it was the verse from Sūrah Maryam: '*Would that I had died before this, and had become a thing forgotten, completely forgotten!*'[2] It was a comfort to know that this thought crossed the mind of our courageous foremother too (﷽).

---

2 *Sūrah Maryam*, 19: 23.

Having conquered the fear twice, I thought I was done. Two labours, blessed with two children and eternally grateful that all three of us had survived. All I needed to do, I would tell myself, was forget the details and the historic fear would just melt away. It worked for a few years, as life became so full of raising them. I did forget. That was until the episode of sprinting out of the Boots perfume department. Out it popped straight away; the folder of memories stored in my head came back with a vengeance.

Mixed emotions hit fathers in other ways too. We went around in a daze for the first week after the positive result. Our heads and hearts knew that this was an incredible blessing, and our gratitude was genuine. I expect you're feeling grateful too. Yet that isn't the whole picture, as I see in your expression. Our thoughts were jumbled; thankful, worried, a portion of guilt about mixed feelings because we knew enough couples around us struggling with infertility and how they would welcome this, nausea and all.

Looking back, we were typical of those overwhelmed, sleep-deprived parents juggling the non-stop needs of the family: cooking, cleaning, laundry, keeping up with the extended family, children's school lives, community work. The tightly packaged days and weeks looked like they would burst at the seams if another human being were to be added. And the guilt of feeling like this, of limiting our thoughts like this, added another layer of confusion. We only snapped out of the daze when my husband's parents visited us. They hugged us as though it was Eid day. Their elation, their happiness and joy were magnetic and pulled us in the right direction.

If you're finding the blue line anything other than joyous, you're not alone, you're not a bad person, or of weak *īmān*. You are human. And we need others around us to help us.

Your steps to seeing the good in this will take their own shape. It could take long strides or short sprints to reach a place of contentment and thankfulness. Step by step, when you put your trust in Allah (ﷻ) you'll be comforted, secure by remembering that He Who is The Provider will '*provide from sources you cannot imagine*'.[3] That brings tranquillity to the heart.

Whether it is mental strength and coping methods, a place to live, physical ability, all of these together, or something else, we need to look for practical help at the same time as trusting in our Lord. He is Our Sustainer. He is *al-Khāliq* – The Creator on Whom our life depended, before we even knew 'life' on this planet.

Well, going back to that blue line, it turned into the toughest pregnancy of the three. Maybe my body had a clue about what was coming and therefore sparked a sense of fear in me from the outset (little did I know a fourth was coming two years later, bringing me back to this waiting room!). There were times during that pregnancy when I cried with exhaustion and the inability to cope with the other two children, then cried some more from being such a 'bad' mother to them with their sibling inside me. All four of us locked in my sinking feeling of inadequacy. Those were the worst days.

---

3   *Sūrah al-Ṭalāq*, 65:3.

And then there were better days. These lasted for several days at a time, where I could carry off being a 'coping mother' and a pleasant 'expecting mother' without upsetting the child-to-be or the children around me.

Very gradually, the better days outnumbered the difficult ones and slowly the 'brain freeze' that I felt at the beginning of the pregnancy improved too. Seeing a friend or two regularly and spending a day at my parent's place now and again helped me. It's different for everyone, I guess, regarding what they need to get through. With my mind feeling itself, I could appreciate the following verses which radiated a warmth of comfort and balance. These verses illuminated the way forward for the rest of the pregnancy:

> *To God belongs the dominion of the heavens and the earth. He creates what He wills [and plans]. He grants female offspring to whoever He will, male to whoever He will, or both male and female, and He makes whoever He will barren. He is all knowing and all powerful.*[4]

> *It is He Who brought you all forth from the wombs of your mothers when you knew nothing; and He gave you hearing and sight and intelligence and affections – that you may give thanks [to Him].*[5]

> *And put your trust in Allah if you are believers.*[6]

Like being thrown a lifejacket in the middle of a rough sea, these Qur'ānic verses took me from remembering His blessings to the safe shores of gratitude and trust. They

4 *Sūrah al-Shūrā*, 42: 49 -50.

5 *Sūrah al-Naḥl*, 16: 78.

6 *Sūrah al-Mā'idah*,5: 23.

reaffirmed that nothing is in our control and that it is God alone Who decides what and when He gives us. I share this with you as we realise the blessings of having another child, but sometimes it's easily forgotten too.

I hope sharing a few of my memories with you will help you at some point. Maybe not this afternoon, maybe not this week, as you are on your own timeline, just like I was on mine.

I know the angst reflected in your eyes is temporary and will pass given time and keeping close to *al-Wudūd*, the Loving One. He is *al-Salām*, the Source of Peace, *al-Wakīl*, the One Who is Relied Upon. Remember that being kind to yourself is finding out what help is out there for you if you continue to struggle – and reaching out for it. Looking after the tree that carries the fruits is vital. It is compassion you deserve.

I'm here for a while today, so I'll leave this letter for you at the reception. I hope you receive it. May your journey to contentment and acceptance give you abundant courage and happiness.

With love,
A fellow mother in the clinic.

3

DEAR MOTHER-TO-BE

From:
Aunty Leylo
Founder of The PCC
(The Pearl Coffee Club)
Buttercup Community Centre
Head in South London
Heart in Somaliland

Our Dear Yusra,

First of all, we miss you!

Yesterday was wonderful. We finally met each other after all these months apart from the coffee club. Even though everyone came, it wasn't the same without you. The tea brews stronger and coffee smells richer when you're helping us out here. We hope the rest of your antenatal appointments will be on a different day. We miss you at the PCC!

Well, with one person after another asking 'where's Yusra today?', I told them you're at your antenatal check-up. We then found ourselves walking down memory lane thinking back of our experiences of pregnancy and delivery. One after the other, as we remembered our pasts, a basket of tales tumbled out.

We might look like just another bunch of elderly ladies but we know how to get round the world through our stories! We went from Morocco to Somalia, then from Pakistan to Bangladesh in just one morning!

Now, as I didn't want you to miss the best stories that were told I wrote them down, as I remembered them over the past week. I've clipped them together for you, to read them when you're next putting your feet up with a cup of herbal tea. I realised when I looked at them together that they are a world away from your generation's life here in England – just about everything's changed! But you're interested in our past and I hope you'll enjoy seeing a bit more of what things were like after giving birth; mostly traditions to make those first weeks calmer.

I must say it's been a delight to write these memories, I haven't written like this since my teaching days.

Asila, Morocco

Nour started off with her baby delivery story from her hometown of Asila in Morocco. Babies were delivered by respected and experienced *qāblah*s (traditional midwives). Two of Nour's aunts were *qāblah*s, so the women in her family were assured of help during their labour and for forty days after. Nour told us how they carried generations of wisdom about natural ways to heal the mother after delivery using traditional remedies. And, of course, wrapped in their aprons were colourful tales that filled the air like the steam from the various potions they mixed. She said she'd heard as many stories as the spices in her grandmother's jars! And she's saving some to tell you, Yusra, over the next months.

What we all enjoyed hearing about was the ceremonies they held for the mother-to-be as they waited for the new-born to arrive. There were herbs to find and pick, oils to prepare and recipes to cook for the 40 days that the new mother was looked after. Nour got us all hungry as she listed the soup ingredients and the buttery, flaky *msemmen* and soul warming slow cooked *rfissah*.

By the time she finished, it was as though we could smell the bouquet of flowers and the oils used for the mother's postpartum care during the *hammām* routine. What lucky mothers! She described some other daily ceremonies; wrapping the mother, massaging her well with olive oil and helping her with feeding the new-born. The most important role relatives played, she remembers, is letting the new mother rest by helping with the other children. And at the end of the 40 days, well even if it was small and simple, they had to have a little gathering to celebrate, singing some folk tunes and enjoying a special dish or two. See if she'll sing one for you, Yusra!

Burco, Somaliland

Well, Nour's memories brought back all the sweet fragrances of Morocco and Aunty Yasmin made us long for the way food was prepared in our beloved homeland of Somaliland. I grew up in the rural part and Aunty Yasmin grew up in one of the big towns called Burco. Most of our customs for the mother and new-born were similar with just a few differences.

One thing was the same for sure; someone – an aunty, a cousin or a sister – would go and stay with the expecting mother just as she was ready to give birth. That was a must! And when there was no one who could go to stay with her, the expecting mother went to stay at her mother's house for the special forty days called *Afartan bax*.

Oh, those times came to life as she remembered how the new mother wasn't supposed to do any heavy housework for the first couple of weeks after birth, focusing on feeding the baby and resting her body. After that she would help with lighter chores. All the big cooking (it was a few families living in the same compound) and washing, cleaning, giving the siblings their baths were all done by cousins or sisters.

The best bit Yasmin shared was the sweet spiced tea – *shah*, the *muqmad* and *odkac* (Somali meat dishes), which was made to strengthen the mother, along with the dates and milk. And at the same time she laughed about how they would scold the little brothers always ready to 'test out' the special food and drinks as they were being made. The emphasis was on making sure the mother was getting the right nutrition as she focused on breastfeeding.

Maraq, a warming soup and *sabaayad* or *kimis* (types of bread) would be the first thing to be prepared every morning. For Aunty Yasmin, the worst part was being forced to drink camel milk. Oh how they wanted her to drink it! But she never could manage it, and after a few days they gave up.

The most comforting memory she shared was knowing there was help with the first baby, the one she was most unsure about; what the different cries meant, how to soothe and wrap the baby and getting comfortable with the nursing. Before her next baby was born, they moved to Holland and she described what a shock it was for her to give birth alone and experience post-delivery loneliness. It was just her and her husband managing.

Everything was tough – understanding how the health system worked, where to buy stuff for a baby and then nursery rules for the elder one. Her husband's workplace was not helpful when she'd given birth. Similar to Rida's memories I'll share, Yasmin soon realised when living abroad in Holland that the women she was nearby had to help each other to survive. They had to *make* their new communities. And getting to know one, then two, then more mothers, they supported each other.

'If I'd known I would be living in Holland three years later, I would have slept the whole forty-days back home after my first! It's another world to have a baby in!' she said energetically shaking her head. Her tale ended with a description of the dinner party, *Afatarn bax*, something we both felt emotional about as I had very similar traditions in my family when I became a new mother. It's not surprising as Yasmin and I come from the same area.

Her memory of the *Afartarn bax* was so good, it's as though she was wearing the soft cream silk gown with the delicate leaf patterns. As though she'd just had her hair done and hands painted with henna. Yasmin remembered how ready she felt to go home when her husband arrived to collect her and their baby daughter, who wore the most adorable dress her aunt gifted her. But once she got back to her routine, all the same headaches with her husband started again. She had us bent over laughing about how she handled that – but I'll stop this note here Yusra, on the high of the *Afartan bax*!

P.S. Yasmin sent me this poem her talented granddaughter wrote. She read it out to us the next week and passed her copy on for you. We enjoyed her reading, feeling the earthiness of it.

Tie Your Waist!

Dhexda xiro!
Dhexda xiro! Tie your waist! My *hooyo* told me.
Caloosha xiro! Clutch your stomach!
Like her mother told her.
Jileeca iska daa! Don't be so brittle!
My *hooyo* told me.
I rolled my eyes.
And wondered why I wasn't allowed to be human.
Why I was being told not to feel.
Dhexda xiro! They told us all.
I bit my tongue and wondered why we were expected to be perfect.
Jeleeca iska daa! They reminded me, I fumed inside and pursed my lips.
Until I grew up and had to start adulting.
'*Dhexda xiro!*' became my maxim.
I tie my waist whenever I fall, to get back up and keep on moving.
Caloosha xiro!
I clutch my stomach and pick up the pieces when the laundry starts to pile and

aimlessness begins to seep into my bones.

Jileeca iska daa!

I tell myself this when the words of a naysayer eat at
my peace of mind.

Dhexda xiro.

Caloosha xiro.

Jileeca iska daa.

My foremothers said.

And they help, show me the way.[7]

Dhaka, Bangladesh

Well after Somaliland, we travelled with Anju – Nani Anju
as you call her – who shared her family's traditions in
Bangladesh (she did stress this was just her in-laws who did
this, not everyone). When she had babies, her mother or
maternal aunt *khālah*, would come and stay at her house as
her parent's house was too small for her and the children.
They would stay about a month and help her with the baby
and all the sores – she had very difficult births, but don't
worry she was fine with enough rest and the right medicines.

In Dhaka, where she lived, there was a *daee*, a local old
lady who came every other day to massage her. The *daee* was a
small old lady with her crooked, tough, experienced fingers.
She would tell Anju her stories from the village while she
rubbed scented oil all over her. Her tales were often about
the hardship of village births due to the lack of trained
midwives. The only clinics were miles and miles away.

Dear Mother: Letters from the Heart

Nani Anju said on the fortieth day her in-laws, where she lived, had a *'chand raat'* – a 'moonlit night' – for the new mother. This was just a traditional name because the mother would stay in her room for those first forty days. They would say she's seeing the moon for the first time after delivering the baby.. That name was an excuse for a big get together, it's not that they didn't see the moon all month! This tradition, which was practised in Anju's in-laws' family included new clothes for the mother and relatives bringing gifts for the baby. The *daee* was the chief guest that night too and expected her dues from the guests as well!

Lahore, Pakistan

You may know that Aunty Rida, as you call her, never had children of her own. Instead, she was a mother figure to her nieces and nephews. As she spent many years studying and then teaching in their hometown of Shahdara in Lahore, she witnessed the births and post-delivery needs of the women in the neighbourhood. In her mother's house there was always two extra pairs of hand to help; loyal home helpers who had grown up in their family. But when her sister got married and moved to her own home, it was different in every way.

And when her first niece was born (hers was among a few families who used the hospital), the only helping hand was the woman who came once a day to wash the floors and clothes. (Well that was similar to me; no washing machines back in those times in Pakistan or Somalia!)

With Rida doing her final exams and their mother

unwell, there was no one to help her sister. She remembers hearing how after each baby, her sister was straight back to the stove and dough making, sprinting between the cries of the new-born and the smell of an over-heated *tawa*. Aunty Rida said it was like a little miracle that her new little niece was such a content baby. As though she knew her mother had it tough and stayed quiet just long enough for her to get chores done.

'Every new mother needs some help' she said, 'so with the next baby my sister made sure she came back to our home where there were more hands holding and caring in the first month.'

Over the years, new mothers in the neighbourhood shed tears on Aunty Rida's shoulder. Being unmarried herself, she listened without making comparisons.

Strung out like the washing lines, their conversations crossed the roof-top while hanging clothes. And it was up there among the kites and the clouds that they'd distribute their tiredness, like portions of seasonal fruit, and concoct reasons to take the baby and stay at their grandmother's house.

With family scattered after the Partition, the women knew their neighbours were the only family they would have, so they supported one another. And Aunty Rida joined in whenever she could, getting ingredients for the *yakhni*, or walking the new-borns up and down the veranda till they grew heavy with sleep and always having a sympathetic ear to hear their daily downs (they didn't share the ups with her!). Rida described some of the new mother's outpourings like a pressure cooker releasing steam...*whoooshhhh*! And then they'd sit back silent and peaceful for a while. That's how she got to know them so well.

So dear Yusra, I know this might seem like another planet we were on all those years ago. The world has spun ahead so fast and some things for pregnant women are easier now than in our time. In other ways, there are new struggles, like some new mothers feeling lonely and isolated, or having to go back to their full routines straight away when they're desperate for more time to recover. I know your family isn't nearby, so I hope your good friends will help out. And don't forget we're not far away for company or help too, you can always come here with the baby for a change of scene. We would love that.

With all our prayers for a healthy and happy pregnancy! See you back at the PCC soon.

Aunty Leylo

4

DEAR MOTHER
FEELING LOW AFTER DELIVERY

From:
A nursery practitioner
A parent with a child in the same *masjid*
Studying maternal wellbeing

Salaam Dear Daania,

You are feeling low and I can't say 'I understand' or 'I've been there', because the truth is, I haven't felt the way you described after childbirth.

But as I've been working in a nursery for years and talking to other people I work with for even longer – midwives, health visitors and a sprinkling of GPs – I've learnt a thing or two about feeling low after a baby's born. And, well, as we see each other dropping our kids off to the same *masjid* class, I thought I'd reach out after you told me you don't feel yourself.

We both know that change is really slow when it comes to our – as in 'mothers' – needs and health in our community. People are so quick at updating their Sky boxes, their phones and getting hold of the latest gadgets. Or they're quick to latch onto educational info about exams and grades and how to get into this school or that one, 11+ tutors, appeals and all that. When it comes to our own health and survival, it's not even on the list, or if it is, it's at the bottom. Our health is important, but it seems to be by-passed most of the time in our community. I suppose we're guilty too, us women don't want to say when we can't cope, like it's embarrassing. But look at it the other way, so many people depend on us, we've got to look out for ourselves and each other.

So, I thought I'm going to do something for a change and start talking about the problems mothers face during pregnancy and after childbirth, and start with whoever I know, like yourself Daania.

We need to say there's postnatal depression and maternal mental health issues for some mothers even before a baby's born. We can't keep leaving them to suffer in silence and keep face in front of everyone, pretending it only affects other people. I think of mothers I've come across who were having a hard time after giving birth and suffering longer than they had to, because they didn't speak up or realise help wasn't far away.

Remember that course I mentioned, the 'Wellbeing During and After Pregnancy' one, that had spare places my nursery manager got contacted about? Since I started it I look out for mothers who've given birth. I listen out if they come into the nursery saying they're not feeling themselves for weeks. Some get so tearful they can't talk about it, but they let on that they've lost all connection with people they know because they can't face anyone. The nursery pick-up is the most they can do. A bit of baby blues is normal, but when it goes on for weeks and even months, then we can't keep ignoring this. The sooner a mother gets help, the better it is for her and the baby.

So, you're not alone Daania. It could be short-term, and some extra support will help you come through and it will pass *in shā' Allāh*. If it's getting worse, please see your GP or health visitor, or a trained person from a mental health charity and reach out for help.

The body goes through a lot during pregnancy, delivery and post-birth, and now I've learnt mothers still go through changes years after delivery. It's only been five weeks since your delivery (your baby daughter's gorgeous (*mashā' Allāh*, what a gem!) and you're running around with household chores, school with the elder sister, then *madrasah*, shops, checking in on your parents. Well, that's all part of life you're telling yourself – if others can do it, why can't I? But when I list it out like that, and you see it in black and white, it's a lot to take on so quickly.

The other evening at the course, the subject was about the physical and emotional toll pregnancy and childbirth takes on a mother. I thought I knew about this but realised I don't know much. I'm like so many others, just carrying on and on with everything and not taking notice of how I'm really coping. It's what we talked about the other afternoon. The instructor gave us a chapter to read about changes to the mothers' brain from the start of pregnancy up to two years after the baby is born. Those changes we're less aware of. I was stunned. I wish I'd known this before. It's fascinating how a pregnant woman's brain prepares her for taking care of the baby's needs. This shows up in the images taken of the mother's brain before pregnancy, and after. Scientists found the neurological changes can help us to better understand perinatal mental health in general.

The other area we looked at and discussed was the difference between normal 'baby blues' and something else more serious. It's common to feel a bit tearful, the instructor said, or irritable and then switch to being happy and content in a short space of time, for two or three weeks straight after delivery. If the baby is having trouble feeding for example, it's an anxious time for any mother no matter how resilient she might be pre-delivery. She made it clear a couple of times that the time to reach out for more help is if you're feeling hopeless and not connecting with your baby; if the tearfulness is prolonged and there's no enjoyment in the baby, just a feeling of being unable to cope. I hope you're not having these symptoms, Daania? Feeling excessively anxious and experiencing a lack of concentration or sleeplessness are other signs, according to the sessions.

I know this might look like a tonne of information, but I'm putting it out here so you can come back to it later. Postnatal depression (PND for short) can start within six weeks after delivery and sometimes much later, even up to a year after the baby is born. The reasons some mothers are more prone to it, they said, wasn't an exact science. I'll just quote you a bit from one of the leaflets: *'There could be several reasons such as previous mental health issues, lack of support after the baby's born, caring for unwell family members, or even a very difficult delivery.'* Or some more severe reasons like a violent partner (our resources called this 'gender-based violence') or big living stresses like housing and financial issues.

They say these are the common factors, but actually someone might not have obvious issues but still be prone to postnatal depression – it's a health condition and we have to start treating it as such rather than thinking it's because the mother's weak or neglectful. The other helpful thing they kept emphasising is that it's an illness that so many mothers will recover from and return to being themselves. I was also surprised to find out it affects fathers too, as they can have similar struggles as the mother. There's now more information available about helping fathers of new-borns too.

I remember feeling like I've got to go back to normal, as everyone expects, like there's an inconspicuous pressure to be seen as coping with everything perfectly. We tend to look at other mothers going back to work soon after the delivery and think we have to function at the same level, even if we're feeling exhausted and run down. But one person's normal doesn't have to be another person's goal.

Working in this nursery I see all kinds of mothers. Some who are just about coping, but get thrown off track when they see other mothers raring to get back into their pre-baby self and create perfect images of their lives for Instagram or Facebook. Most of us aren't looking picture perfect. One afternoon, a couple of weeks after my first baby was born, I remember attempting to put the rubbish out the back door but it took another three hours till I managed to do so! I'd never realised how much time a new-born takes up.

From what other mothers say to me, all of this can stack up and make the average mother post-delivery feel inadequate. It reminds me of what the instructors said during one of our course sessions: 'nobody sees the mothers struggling the most, as they don't come out with a sign on their head to announce it. They're usually at home, out of sight, quite often feeling isolated.'

People in our community can say some strange things after a baby's born, and that doesn't help. I guess you've encountered some strange and unhelpful comments too, but I hope no one's said them to you, Daania. Things like 'Your milk's like water, give the baby a bottle.' Or 'You've gained weight since you had the baby, you used to be so slim.' Or 'How can *you* look after a baby?' The worst comment I came across recently was said to a new mum who just had a relative visit after she delivered a beautiful, healthy baby girl: 'Never mind. If you're lucky, next time you'll get it right and have a boy.' Can you believe people say such things in this day and age? I was fuming. There is no excuse for this.

What's gone wrong in our community? The same people who will lovingly recite pages of the Qur'ān, don't understand what the Divine revelation says about loving boys and girls equally. Neither do they stop and think about their casual comments about skin colour, which makes me so angry. When I visited a friend and her new-born, I was speechless when I heard: 'How beautiful, the baby's so fair, thank goodness, just like the mother.' It's a good job I was speechless or I might have caused trouble at the time. I couldn't believe what I heard. Some people are so brainwashed by this idea that fair-skin means beautiful that you wonder where to start to work on their colonised mind-set. There's no excuse for this. Sorry for the rant! I just wish our community could move on from this.

The same people who are quick to label mothers as inadequate and irresponsible when it comes to their children's behaviour are slow to understand that some of them suffer real illnesses, one of which is postnatal depression.

And it is like there's some superstition that if you educate women about getting help, then it's putting ideas into their heads about developing problems. How twisted is that? No one wants to get postnatal depression, or struggle. This is entirely out of a mother's control.

Even when it feels like no one understands what it's like, it helped me to remember that Allah (ﷻ) acknowledges every single thing a mother goes through in His Revelation: the pains of labour, the early years of nursing a baby and the toll that takes:

> We commanded every human to care for his parents; his mother carried him in pain during pregnancy and breastfed him for nearly two years. So be thankful to Me and your parents, your destination is to Me.[8]

So many mothers don't realise how highly our physical and emotional states are supported in the Qur'ān and Sunnah. There's such a high status for the mother who is breastfeeding, for example. It makes a difference to know that Allah (ﷻ) gives the mother the same status as someone in military service on a battlefield. The tradition of having help from other women to care for the new-born and the mother's needs goes back in history for a good reason – because communities saw it as a shared responsibility to care for a postpartum mother and not leave her to sink or swim.

---

8 *Sūrah Luqmān*, 31: 14.

I hope you have found some of this useful, Daania. There are different ways to seek advice, if you feel the need. Please don't feel alone. Reach out to family, or friends or to us at the nursery. There are plenty of ways we can get in touch with health professionals for you, if that would help. And please remember, I'm not far if you'd like a chat anytime.

With love,
Asma

5

DEAR MOTHER
WHO HAS A CHILD WITH A DISABILITY.

From:
Another mother
In the Sisters' Hall
Jummah in the masjid
All over the world

Assalāmu 'alaykum Dear Sister,

Here we are today, both of us parts of this human jigsaw spread across the *masjid* hall, where we sit, stand and prostrate in physical closeness and emotional detachment.

You come into the *masjid* with a cheerful expression, and I know I'll meet your smile in our momentary interaction. At the same time, I glimpse in your eyes a few seconds of your long journey as a parent. Maybe you feel differently inside and have learnt how not to show it. Maybe, like the rest of us there are days of coping well, days of struggle and days of reflection.

We don't know each other, but I feel I know you because I watch intently as you communicate silently with your child. The way you notice her facial expressions continuously even when you're speaking to another person, the way you respond to the tilt of her face, the flicker of her fingers; these cues that create the unique language between you both. I absorb something I struggle to name; is it a deeper feeling of warmth, a feeling of restored faith in the inherent goodness of human relationships. Your beautiful daughter and you – a profound experience.

Sometimes I try to speak to you, but it only amounts to what strangers say: 'How are you sister? How are the children? I didn't see you last week.' I'm ashamed of how inadequate this is, compared to the value of your presence. I lower my eyes to the small space in front of me; my miniature world that your presence is expanding.

Somehow, between her communication and your responses, your *ṣalāh* flows, from start to completion, in a seamless movement you turn your head to the left whispering the *salām* as though it strokes her arm, reassuring her. She smiles back at you. I guess she's twelve or thirteen years old. I have no idea of the name of her particular needs. What I do know, is that I've just witnessed something that must be named 'the miraculous bond'. How do I explain this? I see you as a blessed woman, with a magnanimous heart; a strong woman. Someone chosen to mother a pure and blessed child. And while I expect you have your own conflicts and inner struggles like we all do, from where I look, I see you as a role model.

I had a very close friend, Urwa, whose daughter, Sana, had additional needs. I remember her struggles vividly. Often, we had similar problems, and we'd off-load to each other what the latest scenario was that made us lose our cool. For her, the physical exhaustion and disturbed sleep caused her lowest points. For me, two fussy eaters and the problems that caused would be the last straw on some days. She had a lot more patience than I did, and was very supportive in my first years as a mother. Urwa migrated, and we rarely saw each other – maybe once in three or four years – and then it became less and less. I still miss her and

Sana and cherish the memories.

You remind me of Urwa; the way you respond to your daughter's needs reflects the resilience you've cultivated through the stages of her growth. Though your challenges will surely be different to hers or mine, I hope you have supportive people in your life.

There are times I wanted to reach out and tell you about the impact of your presence; that it's an honour for the rest of us to be in the same place as you and learn from you. I lack the courage to extend the hand of friendship further with counter-narratives racing through my mind: *Would she want to meet? Would she want me to visit her? Is it offensive to chat generally about our children and not mention the additional physical and mental needs of her daughter? I'm not even sure of what the right terms are because I've heard them all used; special needs, additional needs, differently abled or disabled? The last thing I want to do is say something clumsy that hurts her. Should I ask her outright? Should I ask her to visit me – or would that offend her, as though I don't realise the juggling she must be doing with appointments, therapies, care givers?* And these questions build up barrier after barrier in my head, leaving me here sat in the same spot, and you over there. If we could spend time together, I would hope our friendship would bring a welcome dimension to your life as it would to mine. I hope we would share your child's personality, her likes, her happiness, her challenges, along with my children's ups and downs too.

When weeks pass and I don't see you here, I wonder how it feels for you to belong to our community. In theory you are part of it, but in reality are there genuine opportunities to 'belong', where you feel included? It's easy to identify the *masjid* – that building at that location – to know about events, to see calendar dates come and go without actually finding a place for your family. How much do we include you in the event plans? Do you make friends easily here? Does anyone visit you, not out of sympathy, but to share the everyday exchanges about life? Are you invited to the many off-shoot social gatherings?

If your answer to any of these questions is in the negative, then we as your neighbourhood have failed you and forgotten the legacy of love and care that *Rasūl Allāh* (ﷺ) gave those with additional needs around him. It means we've forgotten how the Prophet of Mercy (ﷺ) organised the marriage of his impaired Companion Julaybib (؆); how he (ﷺ) was concerned about his Companion leading a full life. Julaybib, who was known to his local community as having physical challenges, already had the attention of *Rasūl Allāh* (ﷺ) and that was enough for him. Yet the Prophet (ﷺ) walked inclusion, as well as talked inclusion. He showed us through the way he treated blind Companions, Companions with conditions that hindered their movement and otherwise disabled Companions. He (ﷺ) supported them in finding their role in society. He made space for them. How does our community fare in comparison?

Today I'm grateful for your presence and what it teaches me. I know I can never understand the dynamics of everything you go through, but I hope you can feel a moment of warmth in your heart to know that you are beloved and an inspiration to me long after we leave this hall. Today I take the step of standing up, walking over to you and reaching out.

Your sister in the prayer hall,
Isra
075720123759

6

DEAR SINGLE MOTHER

From:
Najah, friend and attendee at
The Bread & Pastry Masterclass (Level 1)
Thursday evenings

Salaam Dearest Heba,

I know we've only known each other a short while, on our cookery course, (and we never get to finish our conversations), so I decided to write to you. It's about what you told me – your biggest challenge: life as a single mother.

This is new for you.

It was a shock to my system when it happened to me. I wasn't prepared at all. In the beginning I was just trying to survive mentally and physically, battling all the opinions and judgements, befriending that faithful loneliness that comes to stay. That was years ago, thank God. Since I've raised my children as a sole parent, I've learnt a few things along the way, and I don't hesitate to share my experience if I'm asked anything about it. It's not like there are teams of people out there to cheer us on.

I became a single mother through divorce, and so I can only talk about it coming from that experience. Becoming a single mother from widowhood is completely different with its own heartbreaking challenges. I hope there's less of the judgements passed for mothers in such tragic circumstances.

In my case, I wish someone had told me what I'm going

to say to you. I wish someone had been bold enough to sit with me and share what it's like. But I know people get shy to speak up, in case they might offend. I'm glad I know you well enough, even if it is just through our rushed chats in the class. Here's what I didn't finish saying last Wednesday.

The first is to be kind to yourself.

Being a single mother isn't something we dreamt we'd be; no one does. Once we're here though, we need some kindness, to ourselves first and foremost. It's so natural to be flat out protecting our children through the huge effect the parents' break up has on them that we forget we are human too. You don't have to be so hard on yourself twenty-four hours a day like it's a continuous job interview; as though you are getting marks out of ten for everything you do. Kindness to ourselves is taking the time to find help to heal from whatever led to our situation. Kindness is not blaming ourselves for everything that doesn't go right. Kindness is not expecting all the resources to come from within us, but reaching out for our needs. Kindness is making sure we consciously rest, eat mindfully, get some exercise and time outdoors, or whatever helps us.

You're human, so it's ok to be who you are and do the best you can within that, not the best you can in some imaginary fantasy of the 'ideal mother'. She doesn't exist. She never has.

You've got what it takes already, to be a good mother: caring, devoted and present. If the world has made the list for what a 'good mother' is, ten times longer than what it was in the past, then we need to fold that list up and let it fly off somewhere far away. Being a 'good mother' was never that complicated centuries ago. If you're there for your children, no matter what, nurturing them the best you can, then accept you're doing well.

And that takes me to my second point: make that village.

I wish I was told this as bluntly as I'll say it here. You know people plaster the 'it takes a village to raise a child' thing all over Facebook, Instagram and Pinterest? Well, it seems like a nice idea and nothing to do with the reality we single mothers face at first. I thought a lot about it over the years, especially when I struggled to do it all myself. I broke down so many times because it wasn't possible for one body to be in so many places and be so many things for the kids. It just wasn't possible. That's when I'd think most about this village – and wonder, where the heck is it?

The likelihood is you might not be sat in the middle of wonderful elders and co-parents to raise your children with you, but you can definitely go out there and stitch together your own version. That's what I realised: pull together a spider's web of different sorts of people that you can rely on.

It might start with one other mother, then a couple of their friends, a relative if you're lucky to have a helpful one, and then build on that. You can help and lean on each other to survive those tough days. People who live nearby and who aren't clones of each other. Different is good – it's a mix of strengths. The mother who likes staying indoors and the mother who loves being out. One who's a good driver and one who's got the most patience when it rains for a week and you're all stuck inside. By the time we've finished this course, your baking skills will stand out for sure – a strength you can offer!

Slowly but surely, one by one, making our own support network is a positive step. We might get disappointed in between, but we have to learn from those episodes, get back up and keep building our version of a village that works for us.

The third thing is to keep hopeful.

Instead of the many unhelpful and scaremongering comments, I wish someone had given me some hope: that successful, kind and compassionate children are also raised by single mothers. People are only too ready to project doom and gloom for our children on to us. There was so much guilt, fear, and a type of grief for what had changed in all our lives (not all divorce is angry, mine wasn't) that it looked like we were not coping at first. Learning to accept the new normal, gradually takes its toll.

It takes time to live through it day by day; to spar with the negativity until it gets smaller. Bit by bit the creases of hurt disappear as time steams over them. Each week, each day, the emotional scars get fainter. Until the eye can hardly see it: it's ironed out.

Part of the grief and sadness is the fear that gets mixed in. Even if you don't start off with much, people around you will make sure you're afraid for your children's future. It would have helped me keep my chin up if instead someone had said to me great single mothers have raised great men and women that history has recorded as scholars, ḥāfiẓs of Qur'ān, leaders, scientists. A single parent is no less of a parent.

Often the efforts and sacrifices our children witness in us are what builds their character. I wish I had been reassured with this. I'd tried so often to hide my hardships from my children, but looking back I see now that their strength is due to the fact they learnt to survive and find their abilities while still young. Over time, my children became my strength and I'm thankful and proud of who they have become. Please don't let unhelpful voices of misery snatch your hope and joy away from a future you can build.

And well, Heba, there's so much more to say. But for today, I'll end with this. We both have our faith and so we are never alone for a moment. Allah (ﷻ) is with us. He is *al-Fātih* – The One Who opens. He is the Most Trustworthy Who we can rely upon to open doors to sustain us – body and soul – with *rizq* and knowledge. He is the Ultimate Judge over our affairs; we need to keep this attribute alive in our minds daily. How can we feel weak for too long when we remember He is *al-'Azīz* – the Most Powerful – and *al-Raḥmān* – the All-Merciful? We know the challenges won't cease and the difficult days will come and go, but we can strengthen ourselves by knowing that our struggles are supported by the Owner, *al-Malik*, of everyone and everything.

I gave you my number last week, please ring or message me when you're feeling lonely. I'd like to introduce you to a couple of friends when you're ready.

Ma'a al-Salāmah
With much love,
Najah

7

DEAR MOTHER EXPECTING A BOY

From:
Your cousin
Once 'new' mother of a son
Reflecting on that voyage

Dearest Feriha, *Selam*!

I'm still overjoyed from our long phone call and so happy for you all: a baby boy is on his way *in shā' Allāh*. We joke about the generation gap between us cousins, but this is surely the best part for me, when you, younger ones, bring such great news.

I had to write to you straight after our conversation, which was left unfinished (sorry, the electrician got the appointment time mixed up), on the huge subject of raising boys. You're not the first to ask. With three sons, the subject is always in the air for me! Your observations about gender equality and attitude issues we're still facing went a lot deeper than the usual 'how did you get your twelve-year-old to do homework' convo. I'm happy to share my thoughts, but just remember it's only my experience, and every mother's take will be different. At last, this ageing cousin of yours might be useful, Feriha! Sometimes there are advantages to parenting in different generations.

As you asked me to start from where I noticed a difference in attitudes towards girls and boys, I'll start my journey from the maternity ward. Yes, right from there in my case. I guess I'll add a warning here – I have a lot to share, so get comfortable.

I wasn't entirely sure when I woke up, or regained consciousness; there's a fine line between the two. I remember that feeling of relief to wake up with the baby at my side in the dimly lit ward in the depths of the night. It felt as though the rest of the world dissolved around us.

I soon felt more awake once the painkillers wore off. My uterus hurt and my legs felt like lead; I slumped back down, defeated. In contrast, the midwife's assured movements drew an invisible ring of security around me. As she arranged my pillows and my arms in her authoritative style, she announced 'So you have a boy – congratulations. The line will continue. A boy to continue the family name.' I can still hear her regal tone, and see her friendly smile.

Even in that state, I wondered what on earth she was talking about. My sleepy mind kept flipping between half thoughts; had I changed my clothes since the labour? could I feel my toes? what a relief that I could, and they were the one part of me that didn't hurt. And then I was out of it again, in deep sleep.

The post labour brain fog meant I wasn't taking in much. But one phrase stuck in my mind. That emphatic *'the line will continue.'* I had a daughter already, so what did she mean?

I took you back to the maternity ward, Feriha, as that was my first hint on my experience of how people see the value of a son. As you know, I haven't got brothers, so I didn't encounter the attitude first hand. I wouldn't be exaggerating if I said hundreds of hours of conversation later – conversations about raising children in today's world

– I revisited the words of that midwife: *The line will continue.*

After having a baby girl, I was curious about what could be so different. The one thing I did figure out from the first week was the difference in appetite: the feeding, top ups and more feeding was relentless. Gradually over the months I realised, whether it was personality or gender, there seemed to be many more physical outlets needed to burn off this little boy's energy.

Beyond the basics, I realised year on year there were 'systems' that worked for girls but didn't work too well for boys. Particularly when it came to schools – that was another whole tome of discussion and research: how to educate boys and girls to get the best out of them in a holistic way. As part of that awareness, about what does and does not suit boys in the education system, was also waking up to their mental health needs and facing them, unlike the generation before us. In terms of daily life, much of how we raised our sons and daughters was the same – the values, the moral compass, faith and soul consciousness, nurturing their talents. There was no difference between them in terms of the emphasis we placed on these.

It was when I peered into the kaleidoscope of how boys are raised in our community – that immigrant, culturally blended, evolving, multi-identity, spectrum of 'Muslimness' – that I saw the patterns refracted a hundred times more. I think your questions at the end of our phone call were related to this. I came across so many 'norms', so many tales, so many 'Sister, you should never ... ' and 'Sister, listen, if he does this, then ... '

What was I supposed to take and leave? Friends, our relatives, random mothers I bumped into had their issues with sons and an entire universe worth of observations and theories to share. And I started to see that no matter which bit of the mosaic I looked at, there was an indigo streak common to all: the distorted privileges and inherited patriarchy. I hear your 'Yessss', Feriha! To a greater or lesser degree, it was there in every direction.

So I turned to our Islamic heritage and asked how does raising a boy take place in the Prophetic example? Even though the context was vastly different, there must be principles to draw on. What stood out when I started looking into the world of *Sīrah*, was the *way* the Prophet (ﷺ) treated youth generally.

I found many examples of how *Rasūl Allāh* (ﷺ) trusted and respected the young people around him starting with his own daughters and extending out to their growing community. The history of the boys growing up in the shadow of *Rasūl Allāh* (ﷺ), shows that they were given the confidence to think. He (ﷺ) gave them responsibilities according to their abilities. He (ﷺ) gave them space to express their emotions and did not belittle them. He set their sights on the highest ideals of attaining success in the Hereafter and *iḥsān* – excellence – in this world. He (ﷺ) emphasised the importance of the company they keep and the effect this has on a person. He (ﷺ) set boundaries connected to *taqwā*. He (ﷺ) cried and laughed with them. He (ﷺ) ate and travelled with them, beside them. He (ﷺ) nurtured them with his time and attention. He (ﷺ) showed his love to them and corrected them when needed. These were the qualities that nurtured boys into men. The expression 'teenager' hadn't yet been invented.

Of equal importance were the answers I found about the role model for gender relations in the beloved *Rasūl Allāh*'s (ﷺ) example whereby the faith and status of a young man were not unjustly raised above the faith and status of a young woman, ever. I found my compass reinforced; 'Do treat your women well and be kind to them for they are your partners and committed helpers,' said the noble Messenger of Allah (ﷺ) in his very last sermon, reminding humanity of that partnership and respect.

Weeks swam into months, months waded their way into years and those years piled layer upon layer and made me question that midwife's congratulations. Raising our daughter was equally important. In some ways it felt more urgent to ensure her status was reinforced to make it strong because we knew the world could be a harsh place for girls.

As my ears became attuned to the 'raising boys' narratives, I looked for equity between nurturing boys and girls, but instead I heard much to the contrary; stories of unbelievable privilege and chauvinism, laments of injustice. These weren't the only narratives, but they were still too many. And to make matters worse, there were too many examples of what the privilege and complex social causes turned into: 'going off the rails', 'directionless', 'lacking motivation and lost'. As the years progressed, I did my best in my own home to change the story about raising privileged boys. The practical daily realities, though, showed me time and again that fast-changing social pressures are a mighty force. Parental influence alone can't guarantee success. How many parents around me flung their hands up in the air in despair – their boys were liabilities to society – their struggle was tangible. This minority was growing, and I continued to search for what we could collectively do to help raise balanced and content boys. Simplistic statements like 'they follow the parents' example' were insufficient to explain the increasingly complicated issues I saw around me.

Stories of Prophets Ya'qūb (عليه السلام), Nūḥ (عليه السلام), and Ādam (عليه السلام) in the Qur'ān, when contemplated at length, finally shed light on the chaos I witnessed. Parents can model what's right. Surrounding community can contribute and signpost, and every responsibility can be carried out by the family. Yet still, this world of tests unfolds as we are promised it will, through our children, our health and our wealth.

It wasn't all doom though, Feriha. I focused on this as it's what we started to discuss. Along the way, there were scenes that restored my hope. I saw many talented boys grow into inspirational young men – men with integrity and motivation. Boys who reached their potential and contributed to their families and community. Young men who struggled with their health or circumstances and faced their challenges head on, pushing forward, bit by bit. Community mentors, where troubled teens returned as sage adults to lead the way. These examples lit the path and we raised our son with caution and courage, steering through all the conflicting messages to some clarity. The tiny person the midwife handed me – this unique soul God assigned to my womb – would need raising in a way that suited him. And that was one part of the clarity: that along with timeless wisdoms and beliefs, the methods of nurturing our boys and getting the best out of them will differ. They *should* differ, just as our distinctive fingerprints are testimony that no two people are the same.

I met fellow parents across the length and breadth of the land trying to figure out the same things I've mentioned. You might have been too young back then to know that the work I did in those years brought me in contact with families from all backgrounds. At one of my sessions, a group were sat around a table discussing general issues that affect children's upbringing today. It didn't take long for them to stop on the subject of raising boys. A mother of six children shook her head when the teenage years were mentioned. Her rising emotions were evident as she tightened her shawl around her, reigning in words, words and more words on her experience.

At the first opportunity to share her thoughts, she jumped in and spoke as though her heart finally got the release it had been waiting for. Like a hundred spools of string unravelling, tumbling across the table, unfettered by commas, dashes or stops, all in one go, she spoke: 'We raise our boys to be celebrities, like they are so special, like the ground they walk on is blessed. *Eh*, this is the problem.' She pointed at an empty space on the table, 'This ... this is the problem. They are nothing special. They are standing on our head and making our life like rubbish. Too hard. It's too, too hard, sister. But it is all of them, all the community's fault to make them like this. Yah.'

There was unanimous agreement with all heads nodding. She continued: 'I tell my boys now, go, go and pick up your bedding in the morning from the sofa. Wash your cups. But you know, it's in their blood not to help and they start complaining. But I want to change them. I shout, "You pick up the bedding, you hear me."' There was unanimous agreement again.

Sitting to her left, the quiet, tall mother who had propped up her nursing baby and herself on a chair far too small for the both of them raised her hand and opened her mouth simultaneously, as though she was demonstrating a new exercise: 'And the men, this is the men they become, like some lord of the town. Like when they walk, they will bring the air for us to breath. But they're doing nothing sister. Nothing. Drinking coffee, passing time or they are just sleeping. They don't do anything to help.'

I learnt far more than what was on the agenda that morning. I learnt that no matter what the languages, they were speaking one tongue of frustration. Some came from a complex history; where the seeds were sewn in another land, brutally uprooted and replanted into foreign soil. Problems grew without the luxury of a botanical expert to tame the unruly branches and nurture the fruit bearing trees. The passage of time brought a generational shift to solve those difficulties, and now you see the role models courageously emerging across our communities. A new generation dealing with challenges, tilling the land to cultivate according to the new climate they face. Now these young men are the experts and need to be heard.

Whether a mother admitted to struggling or not, their

stories often boiled over into the everyday exchanges I had; conversations seeking solutions that happened in corners of the *masjid*, in cafes, around a friend's kitchen table, through the windows of parked cars waiting for a school club to finish. Each year, something was added to the list of challenges, but by then I'd figured out how to map all these experiences in my head.

I found comfort in the guiding principles from the life of the Messenger (ﷺ); demonstrating courage, integrity, humility, hard work, a soft heart and, above all, an unwavering God-consciousness no matter what lay ahead. Focusing on the Qur'ān – *al-Furqān*, The Criterion or Differentiator – I felt reassured by the roles of believing men and women, as allies who:

> ... *support each other; they order what is right and forbid what is wrong, they keep up the prayer and pay the prescribed alms; they obey Allah and His Messenger. Allah will give His Mercy to such people: Allah is Almighty and Wise.*
>
> *Allah has promised the believers, both men and women, Gardens graced with flowing streams where they will remain; peaceful homes in Gardens of everlasting bliss; and greatest of all – Allah's good pleasure. That is the supreme triumph.*[9]

These principles secured a framework for us; sons, daughters and parents.

Out of the woods now I realise, looking back, just how limited parents are if they try to do this job alone, and how much rides on the collective effort to support our

---

9   *Sūrah al-Tawbah*, 9: 71-72.

boys. With time and experience, confusion gave way to confidence by holding on to the Divine message. Whether it's a son's role and responsibility in society or family ties, or their emotional and mental wellbeing, or the all-important career choices, our faith anchored us as a family. With time and knowledge, we learnt to differentiate between making thoughtful changes for a new generation and swallowing dubious ideas that confuse.

And with that, our journey of raising sons and standing back to see their natural place in this world became that bit easier, happier and more enjoyable. Thank you for asking about this, Feriha, I've never put it down on paper before like this. Maybe we should write to each other. Write me something before you have the baby, please! I want to read your thoughts on all this too.

Love and hugs from your favourite cousin,
Cemil

8

DEAR MOTHER
FEELING PRIMARY SCHOOL STRESS

From:
A fellow parent
Primary school playground
By 9.30 am

Hi there,

I stand to the left of the playground gate. I choose not to talk to anyone. Can't do daily small talk anymore. I've run dry.

Life changes, things happen. I prefer to keep myself to myself. People say you can't pour from an empty cup and I feel as though even the clouds have dried up.

Yesterday as I ended up under the rain shelter, I overheard you mention feeling overstretched and exhausted. Overwhelmed with the needs of children, the education system, the news, being a visibly Muslim mother – it's like standing in the centre of a traffic junction where the signals have failed, and chaos is the highway code. At least you expressed this to a friend. Most of us just try to avoid dwelling on these thoughts. We bury them.

I understand how you feel. That's why I'm writing to you.

How could you not feel distressed? It's entirely expected, if anyone stopped to look at what we mothers face. Like all parents, we've got the *à la carte* menu of challenges to taste. Then, having our *dīn* as our priority, adds a whole new layer to the mix. Also, part of that mix now, whether we like it or not, is to understand world politics and answer random questions. I mean, when I'm picking up my kid in the playground, what's that got to do with a dictator or an invasion a million miles away?

There's no choice. We're expected to have an answer ready. But we're struggling like all the other parents. We can switch it all off, every news channel, but the news still comes right back at us. 'So, what age were you allowed to go to school?' a parent asked me the week the latest troubles in Afghanistan became headlines, again. I came here from Bangalore at the age of eight and both my parents have degrees. What on earth did that parent mean by 'allowed to go to school'? I hope you don't get comments like this too often.

Aside from the parents' comments in the playground, we have our own expectations to keep up with. How much do we manage in just one morning; household needs, grocery stops, keeping the kids safe (accidents even at home, never mind elsewhere), that place value maths sheet, the lunch box. On top of that, we put time into their spiritual needs. Nurturing their soul is part of the equation. Establish the *ṣalāh* with them and for them, make it mean something in their lives. Being the constant moral compass, in a world where the needle spins relentlessly.

We see to their physical health, of course. Walking the younger two to school is the easiest bit. Playing in the park I can handle too. But it's the host of sporting activities to figure out that I get tied in knots about ...

Sorry, I've digressed, off-loading my own frustrations.

I understand your feeling of being overwhelmed. Sort out one issue (like the catalogue of lunch-time problems one of mine's just had) and sure enough, up pops another and then another. By this point it's not worth looking things up. The last time I went online for help, all I found was how much damage I might have caused because of the distance between the cot and our bed, and the formula milk feeds I gave to get through the night.

I understand our feeling of being overwhelmed. I don't know if feeling guilty affects you the way it affects me. Some of us spend hours mentally punishing ourselves about all the wrong ways we've done things when we come across another 'parenting expert' who shares his or her theories. Somehow, I don't remember these characters, 'Guilt' or 'Doubt', featuring so prominently in either of my grandparent's domestic stories. Maybe they were surrounded by a similar value system that made it easier to parent. I'm not saying they got it all right. It would have helped if they stopped to think about some of their decisions. One difference I do realise between their generation and ours is that we've got heaps of 'parenting styles' trying to get our attention and it can all get too much.

Sometimes being here in the school playground can set us off on a downward spiral of feeling inadequate. That's half the reason I gave up the chats. Clubs, classes, coaching, tuition, levels and sub-levels, sets and bands can entangle our minds into a quiet state of panic.

I overheard you describe a friend in tears when they got home from the morning school run. A hard working, caring mother in tears, releasing the stress she felt. Whether she had other things going on, or it was playground peer pressure, we need to remember that our children will develop on their own timeline. And they'll learn the reality that we're imperfect people making our best effort.

It's Autumn term, so here goes the Harvest Festival basket extravaganza. We put in effort to make them excellent. Fine. We contribute to a care home. That's good. But the award-winning expectations we place on ourselves – why? We're ambassadors of our faith, that's why. At 8.45 am, at 8.51 am, at 12.30 pm and at 3.30 pm – basically at any random time – we represent it. We've got a subconscious neon sign on our foreheads with a load of justifications crammed on to it: I'm a good citizen, upholding FBV,[10] not the mother of a kid running off to join anything anywhere, not oppressed or oppressing, not, not, not ...

What must it feel like to be 'a mother', and *just* that?

Is it any wonder you feel shattered? Is it any wonder we feel a global fatigue? And what is the exhaustion from? Perhaps you know the answer deep down. It's not common to name these things, but I will. It's from the mental and physical work of looking at one thing in ten ways and trying to score in five separate goals all at once. One of those goals is called 'representation', and that alone is a mountain of responsibility on your shoulder – on our shoulders – the shoulders of any mothers belonging to the misrepresented.

This 'representation' goalpost is insane to any logical mind, but we all fall under its pressure daily. Neither you

---

10 Fundamental British Values. These are defined as the values of the rule of law, democracy, individual liberty and 'mutual respect and tolerance of those with different faiths and beliefs.' https://www.gov.uk/government/news/guidance-on-promoting-british-values-in-schools-published (2014)

nor I can represent 1.8 billion fellow Muslims who share the same faith. We can do our best as individuals, but that's quite different to feeling like we need to represent all Muslims every morning at 8.50 am and every afternoon at 3.30 pm. The pressure from this alone is draining.

If only there was someone who could catch us in these moments of pressure and remind us: you are not responsible for all of this. Your best effort as a parent is enough. Enjoy these primary school years, relax with them more than measure your performance. Limit what your senses are exposed to and save the best part of your soul for your loved ones. Recognise that maintaining a stable, safe, loving home is all it's about. The rest will come and go with time.

It is wishful to think that someone would give us this message on those days of feeling overwhelmed – so I'm writing to you in the hope we support mothers who need to hear this.

We need to stand far back and take another look at what we do and *why* we do it. Who is putting these demands on us? Clarity comes when we wipe away the excessive messages that have scrawled across our minds regarding what a 'good Muslim mother' does and replace it with a kinder reality.

Our reality. Our parameters, that we set. Our priorities, that we choose. Our selves, that we invest in. *This* will be our reality.

With understanding and respect,
From a mother who knows burnout too well.

9

DEAR MOTHER
MISSING HOME

From:
A fellow migrant Mother
In transit
Placed but displaced
Permanent resident
Temporary ties

Ayesha,

Here we are sat in the transit lounge thanks to a cancelled connecting flight. There's not much to do in the dead of the night but be patient until we reach our destination, our home, *in shā' Allāh*.

I was so engrossed in hearing your story about moving overseas, until that seat change fiasco! So, I've taken the liberty to share some thoughts about my move too. I understand how you feel, time away has taught me certain realities too.

Like you, I too am aching for the familiarity of the land of my birth. The sand, the soil, the raindrops that quenched me and continue to swirl in my veins searching for their source. It feels as though my homeland's earth, water and air are my centre of belonging.

When I think about home, associations fill my mind. Home was another sound. The heightened voices and passion in the fish-seller's argument, assuring the neighbour he did not overcharge her when her daughter paid him last week. Home was the cadence of their battle.

Home was an indescribable aroma of people and grains, stale petrol, pungent berries and the town's stresses carried in the evening breeze through the mosquito netted doors.

Home was where daybreak broke through the windows with distinct rays.

That was home.

I miss the unannounced visits of the neighbourhood elders. One in particular, who would stop by because of her aching joints and aching desire to tell my mother what the Malik family's eldest son, Afzal, told the barber.

The memory makes me smile when I sit alone, reminiscing. Those local incredible tales! This one started with the barber who told his brother, whose wife told her mother, that he (Afzal) was soon planning to travel across the border in search of better opportunities. That he would do so on his own steam by setting off one night, without telling his family, and simply never return until he gained the status he deserved. And the best part was that Afzal told the barber he planned to do this secretly; he was a man now and didn't need anyone's advice. *That* was the ache she came to relieve herself from in the midday heat. 'A fool since his youth!', she declared at the end of her report, with an accomplished expression. It was a tale worth climbing the stairs up to the apartment for.

I end up laughing when I recall her speed in sharing the news that would make any city network connection shrink in comparison. Now I miss her too. Back then at home, her presence was something I escaped from, into my bedroom. What I would give now for that familiarity and warmth that swept in with her and her predictable refusals of iced tea only to drink three glasses while telling her stories.

That was home.

Unlike the way most of your immediate family migrated soon after you, I miss my family that are mostly still in the same city. Some members have moved on too; relationships shift and I've accepted that things are no longer the same. But for those I am in touch with, the love and affection between us are only partially retrieved through the cold screens of our devices. This longing was raw in the first two or three years, but it has a pattern now.

Now it is a different longing. I'm surprised by how it has evolved. It's well over a decade in this foreign land: home, children, neighbours, networks and kind people locally, but still, something is missing. 'That's your home now', my sister reminded me over our most recent call, sensing my mood from my unspoken words.

How do I explain to her this place is becoming less of a home as the years unfold? It's just as you described about the way our perspective changes. How do I explain that as I travel down life's road, my heart hurtles backwards? Instead of my attachment to the homeland diminishing, it increases. That rug in my hallway, those tablemats, the tea set and cushion covers I brought back from my last visit, no longer fill the empty gap that is longing to be filled by the land of my birth.

When you mentioned the connections between your children and your homeland, that brought so many thoughts to the surface. It's not something I've shared before. As I watch my children growing into young adults, carving their own identities, the question of their ancestral heritage surfaces regularly as they figure out who they are. There's a need to hold their roots in their hand and decide which direction they will grow in. That's mostly how I see my eldest developing, the other two are too young to be concerned.

Even though I'm older and should be wiser, I'm still looking for answers to the ancient question, 'Who am I?' My mind drifts some afternoons, as I wonder: do I express myself like my adventurous grandmother? Her stories of youth are no longer found in the crumbled walls of the courtyard that once witnessed her escapades. Do I retreat from situations like that 'taboo' unnamed uncle I've never seen but only heard about; the one who was last seen in a taxi heading to the seaport and then disappeared?

When I look beyond myself, displacement and movement are common all around us, whether we've moved by choice or not. I remember the Islamic studies lessons in my teens, about the *Hijrah* from Makkah to Madinah. Our teacher, may Allah (ﷻ) grant her *Jannah*, was passionate about sharing the teachings from this historic move. 'Reliance on Allah (ﷻ), resilience in difficulty, resolve to take action,' she would say. I miss her. People have always moved from land to land, uprooting and grafting their lives to another place. As you said, it brings strength and resilience, as well as challenges.

Maybe it's this stage of raising children. When our own past and current efforts of raising our own children merge, they bump into each other and jostle for a way ahead. From birth we learnt a certain register of our parents' voice, a certain way elders, strangers or families were addressed. This education started well before textbooks were introduced into our lives. I look back at how simplistic my understanding of language was when my husband and I moved. We thought by keeping our first language alive in our home, we would preserve our culture. We weren't prepared for the fast-changing value system which empties everyday language of the things we took for granted, like *ḥayā'* and *shukr*.

Growing up back home was no idyllic childhood. There were bad influences, negative peer pressures and just as many avenues to go down self-destructive paths as there are here. But they were *different*. Somehow, the elders had a quiet confidence with the good and the bad there. They knew what led to what. We knew the areas of our town: the ones to avoid, the ones where you must go with company even at 12 in the afternoon. People's faces were familiar maps, which were read instantly.

Here, I struggle to apply that intuition – because as I work it out, the game changes, again. When my teenage son talks to me, I catch myself staring through his eyes to see into his soul. Born in this new land, I want to know how the invisible side to my children is developing: their ideas, their aspirations, their heart – what's happening to it all? There is much more to all this than simply knowing some cultural do's and don'ts. Several layers more.

> So, I miss home.
> You miss reading ancestral faces.
> I miss hearing regional dialects.
> You miss being in the know.

I miss the comfort of family.

You miss being a majority – and not squeezed into a 'minority'.

I miss the man who sells the 7Up bottles and the woman who wraps the buns at the stall.

You miss the ornate fabrics left locked in the steel wardrobe.

I miss that poetry collection I left on my grandfather's bookshelf.

We are 'others' now, in another land, with our 'othered' children.

And it's in this 'otherland' that we mother. We roam in a maze to find ourselves. We want to march ahead of our children and lead; but which signposts do we follow?

Like our ancestors, we will find our way, re-settle ourselves and move ahead. There is no alternative. Maybe our children will show us new ways of being, new tomorrows in a language they'll create.

When I stand back from it all – from borders, and visas, from postcodes and exchange rates – I take comfort in the closeness of Our *Rabb* in our lives. No matter where we are, His earth will sustain us and His sky protects us.

While our hearts ache for worldly connections, remembering *Rabb al-Mashriq wa'l-Maghrib* (the Lord of the East and the West) gives me confidence to make the best of my second home.[11]

---

11 *Sūrah al-Shuʿarāʾ* 26: 27.

I'm glad we met on the plane and I'll treasure your story that you shared with me. This delay turned out to be useful, it gave me the chance to write and deliver this to you by hand!

Transit is an apt place to write. Neither here nor there, just in-between.

With you in spirit,
Yusra

10

Dear Mother exploring 'hijab' for her daughters

From:
A fellow attendee at the Study Circle
Mother of daughters,
Once a teenager
Who chose to wear the hijab
Still wearing it now

Salaam Dear Muneera,

It was great to see you yesterday – our monthly study circle and social is a staple of the month, I look forward to it for days ahead. Isn't it funny how our best discussions are impromptu? They sprout from a question, a comment or even a sigh.

That article Salma mentioned after the circle raised the 'red herring hijab topic', again. Another one of *those* articles about Muslim women's clothes, written by someone with no real experience or knowledge. Just an opinion in the paper playground to run around in. It's always the visible that gets attention, whereas the invisible inside our hearts and minds is overlooked.

When Kauser said she's glad her daughter wanted to wear a scarf when she turned seven years old, I saw you wince. I recognise that particular silence. I mulled over the things that were said and decided I'd share some thoughts with you.

One of the ladies began to explain she felt it was too young and not serving the purpose it's for, but she got interrupted and we didn't hear what she had to say. I'm picking up from there. While there's a dozen articles on every platform imaginable about modest dress and the semantics of 'khimār' and 'hijab', I'm going to focus on one thing: how we, mothers, who wear the hijab, approach the subject with our daughters. Apart from having raised daughters who are adults now, I'm drawing on what I've seen working in a girls' school for the past couple of decades.

Context is vital. And context is usually missing from these discussions. As with all of the sacred text, we hold each *āyah* in esteem for what it is: a living miracle, a sign, a message, a proof from our Creator. We learn from them instructions, reminders, warnings, messages of hope and reassurance, lessons from history and so on. One of the main *āyāt* on hijab is preceded by a verse addressing men's modesty first. And for women, the emphasis is about being protected from the unwanted attention. That's the first bit of context that gets overlooked.

The other thing is the *āyāt* relating to hijab/khimār are also few in number, compared to those about our personal living, for instance. The state of our hearts, the uncompromising need for honesty, remembrance of our Creator, humility and modesty, affirming the Hereafter, are just a few examples of repeated themes. I know I'm picking subject matter randomly here. But the point is, these *āyāt* about our 'outer' – about what's visible – are very few in comparison to the verses about our inner being. That doesn't make them any less important, but it helps with context.

So, when we're having discussions about hijab with our daughters, we need to reflect the position it has in our sacred revelation. Sometimes it feels like the fabric on the head and the length of the clothes is all there is to our faith. What a tragedy! Our community compounds this problem with lazy categories too. 'Does she wear hijab?' casually asked in a hundred different situations, as though it's the standard bearer of one's heart and *īmān*.

My other pet peeve is whenever the word 'struggle' is used in a public talk, the only example wheeled out by the speaker is 'The Hijab Struggle', as if people don't struggle with the dozens of diseases of the heart. It's always the outer that gets the attention! And to add to the mixed messages we're putting out there, the media machine does its bit too. It is obsessed with the hijab, niqāb, burka and any other label, as it spills out unchecked rivers of ink over what Muslim women wear, right beside casually objectifying women's bodies throughout its advertising.

To put the hijab in context is important, as our daughters are going to encounter the ways people politicise, or overemphasise, or erase the role of hijab. As long as we are clear on its role in our daily living, we can help our daughters keep the balance, whether they choose to wear it or not. Not getting into the subject of governments and hijab. Using the liberty of them being letters and not khutbas or essays.

Another point, Muneera, that's not as straightforward as context, is an awkward one: peer pressure. You and I both know exactly what I mean. Even within ourselves, the subject of peer pressure and our acts of worship can be a bitter mix. Usually, we can quell the noise of it in our heads by checking our intention that our acts of worship are done purely for the pleasure of God, and not with anyone else in mind.

When it comes to hijab though, there's an obsession in some communities; a hushed comparison, as we've heard in some circles of mothers (certainly not all) that the younger a girl is when she incorporates hijab into her daily wear, the better.

We know it's common and natural that young children copy their mothers and women around them in wanting to dress similarly. Donning a headscarf now and then for young girls is quite predictable imitating – like carrying a purse, or wearing jewellery is. This is different to enforcing it on a six-year-old because of the 'they need to get used to it' reason. For families who choose to this, that's their choice. But you shouldn't feel pressured or guilty if you're not doing the same. I think that was what yesterday's discussion might have done.

It's true there are many acts of worship we involve young children in. They join us in *ṣalāh*, often from a young age, and start a few hours of fasting that grows with their years. And we celebrate their progress! We encourage them to grow good habits from a young age, whether it's giving charity or caring for the environment or showing generosity to a neighbour. And that's the argument used for making the hijab a part of their dress: a good habit.

Ultimately, it's the relationship our child has with their Creator that is the most important thing to nurture and protect. If an outward act of worship is brought into daily life in too heavy a way, it can break the delicate bridge we, parents, are building with *al-Ra'ūf, al-Raḥīm*, The Kind, The Most Merciful. And to jeopardise this link because of social peer pressure is the last thing we want to do.

What's happened to us as a community that the status of a young girl's hijab journey gets more urgent focus than the heart and mind – which are addressed time and again, by our Creator?

The difference is of course the former is seen, the latter isn't. How much do we compare between people on the basis of the inner levels of humility, gratitude, *ḥayā'* (modesty), being charitable, patient or placing trust in Allah(ﷻ)? Of course, we don't and hopefully never will. So why judge or feel pressurised by others when it comes to an item of our clothing? It's time for us to raise the bar of thinking if we want to align ourselves to what He prioritises.

I hope we can support our daughters' understanding of *ḥayā'* as part of their spiritual growth, which brings security and comfort! The challenges will come from society about their dress, as they have come for us, so I hope we aren't the ones to add to those prematurely.

A young person who develops a long and lasting relationship with *ḥayā'* and hijab does so as a result of her relationship with God. Any other motivation will eventually wear thin, as there are too many pressures against wearing the hijab out there in the world to withstand. But the firm foundation of *taqwā*, God consciousness, is the only tool that will survive. Which brings me to where it all starts: the heart. The core of the 'hijab topic', is the heart. How well are we weaving the strongest heartstrings with our young girls towards loving and knowing their Lord – I'm not directing that at you, Muneera, but 'us' the collective?

As for those articles and soundbites online, well, we've ingested those for years. It's no longer worth wasting our energy on refuting them; they will continue to be the 'red herring' dangled by spectators who analyse our entire faith and tuck it into the hem of their chosen fabric. What matters more is how we're fulfilling our responsibility to our children, male and female. And the 'dress' bit is always a tough one in the community because it's the visible part.

With love and a good eye for soft cotton scarves,

Your friend who's lived through the 'hijab chronicles' for three decades!

Hina

11

DEAR MOTHER OF TEENS PRE-RAMADAN

From:
A secondary school teacher,
'Co-parent' to dozens of teens
Informal counsellor to parents
Your local secondary school
Every Ramadan

As-salāmu 'alaykum wa-raḥmatullāhi wa-barakātuh,

Let's keep this short as you hear enough pontificating from every direction on how to:

> discipline,
> teach,
> guide,
> empathise with,
> relate to,
> befriend,
> let go of,
> hold on to,
> avoid conflict,
> set boundaries,
> protect
> your teenage son or daughter.

I know you don't need more of the same. Not today as you organise your family's life for the coming blessed month of Ramadan. So, let's cut to the chase: where do you stand in relation to your teens' experience of Ramadan?

There are two things that come to mind after talking to parents for years, these are expectations and responsibility. We always want the best for our children and students, and that leads us to having very high expectations. Their fasting, understanding of the Qur'ān and their relationship with Allah (ﷻ) sit at a different place on the timeline to ours. Our stage of life is much further ahead. We've developed our relationship with Ramadan in our own way over years.

There are some young people, still teenagers, who will exceed their parents in all areas of Ramadan; the spiritual and the communal. That's inspiring *ma-shā' Allāh*, but I'm not addressing those parents – all five of them (judging from my experience) won't be reading this letter anyway. Apart from this exceptional bunch, the majority of teens struggle with their sleep, the length of the summer fasts, the need to study and sit exams, the additional *'ibādah*, the change of routine. These are the common challenges, and they have only gotten worse for many of our students since the world has been through the pandemic. There's a complex effect the lockdowns have had on children of all ages, and I hope Ramadan will bring them peace, rather than pressure.

Most young people struggle with making a spiritual connection.

When we think about what we expect of them as young souls, and of ourselves, it is worth thinking back to how we formed our personal connections to this month of mercy. Times have changed too quickly! Ramadan in our youth happened when there was little 'hype' online. There were books detailing the *aḥkām* of the month, a few talks or *ḥalaqah*s and one or two Muslim channels to hear the *adhān*.

And how could I forget, there was 'Radio Ramadan' to keep the community spirit alive and entertained! Our experience of the month grew primarily from inside us, with these few external aides to help along the way.

The teens of today are seeing a million fast and attractive messages about Ramadan in highly curated, visually stunning ways, as part of complete marketing plans for the month of the Qur'ān. Ramadan and both Eids are fast becoming hyper-commercialised. Everything with 'Ramadan' stuck in front of it is up for sale, from cooking oil to reflective journals to jelly sweets. At the same time, today's youth are fortunate to have access to an abundance of good quality Islamic learning resources to help them before and during the month.

For them to wade through all the noise and hype, they need some help to see Ramadan for what it really stands for: a month of *taqwā*, of opportunities to grow closer to Allah (ﷻ) and His Divine message addressed directly *to* them.

If there's one thing we can do, it's softening our 'lofty' spiritual expectations and helping them open their eyes to the month as an opportunity to take small steps to build their relationship with Allah (ﷻ). We can help them make '*so that you may be mindful of God*' (2: 183) the primary focus.

Instead of prescriptive measurements and boxes that must get ticked daily to please us, the adults, we can aid them by highlighting the ethos of the month well before it starts, and allowing it to sink in. There are several messages of connection our teens can pick out from this *āyah* to connect to the real purpose of the month.

It was in the month of Ramadan that the Qur'ān *was revealed as guidance for mankind, clear messages giving guidance and distinguishing between right and wrong. So any one of you who is present that month should fast, and anyone who is ill or on a journey should make up for the lost days by fasting on other days later. God wants ease for you, not hardship. He wants you to complete the prescribed period and to glorify Him for having guided you, so that you may be thankful.*

[Prophet], if My servants ask you about Me, I am near. I respond to those who call Me, so let them respond to Me, and believe in Me, so that they may be guided.[12]

Responsibility is the other issue. As a teacher, I can see the effect of taking responsibility – or not – on their outcomes. As a professional, it is easier to detach myself and watch them take account for their actions. I guess it is harder being a parent. Just like us in our youth, your teen son or daughter is responsible for their own actions, as a result of their choices. Their choices may be good ones, or not so good, but they have to *own* their choices. How they make decisions is going to depend on their personal maturity and many other factors. Naturally, parents and teachers expect them to take responsibility for some things in their life.

If they chose to fast mechanically, counting down the days till it is over, then that is what they are responsible for. That might be all they can do at this stage of life, or it could be that it's all they aspire to right now. Please accept this. As a parent you may have done everything from their birth onwards to engender a sense of spirituality within her or

12 *Sūrah al-Baqarah* 2: 185-186.

him, hoping that by young adulthood all your investments would bring back mature returns on their part to make good decisions. But we know it is never that straightforward.

If this Ramadan is not the time to reap the harvest of your input, then don't despair and blame yourself. There are plenty of people with nothing to do who will blame you anyway, variously remarking 'you've done too much for them' or 'you did too little' or 'they were micromanaged' or 'you were too distant from them'. From where some critics stand, it's a lose-lose situation. So don't heap more guilt on yourself. You are doing the best you can. We teachers do the best we can. They are where they are. If they inch forward or not during Ramadan, that's their souls' expedition.

We can support them, guide them, demonstrate through our actions and facilitate the good for them, but we can't 'do' their spiritual growth for them. Ramadan is ultimately about growing nearer to our Sustainer. And just as *al-Hādī* has guided us on our journey, trust that He will surely guide our teens' hearts too.

Maʿa al-salāmah,
Miss El Hadad
A teacher working between teens' challenges and parents' passion.

12

DEAR MOTHER
LIVING WITH PAIN

From:
A mother waiting for test results,
Reading your blog
Afraid

My dear sister,

Today I read your blog and wondered how I got to this place; thousands of blogs and sites out there, but such is our *rizq*. We receive these blessings through a link shared, an icon tapped, and I entered your world momentarily. It was a privilege, an eye-opener, a heartbreaker, food for the soul – all in one. I guess we find what we are seeking. As I've just had a host of medical tests done and am waiting for results, my subconscious drifting online led me to a mother living with a long-term condition. It must be a way our souls prepare us, helping us, just in case this is what is waiting around the corner.

To read of your long-term health problems alongside caring for your own children – being a mother, a wife, a daughter – stopped me in my tracks. When life becomes one appointment after another, one more restriction, one more type of pain management, one more uncertainty, I imagine, as you say, it wears you down into a version of yourself that's hard to recognise.

It sounds as though dealing with a long-term condition actually becomes two or three conditions: first it's the diagnosed health issue, second it brings a psychological challenge and third is dealing with what it does to relationships. All three rotate in their orbit, stars strung together around your life shining a torchlight onto parts uninvited.

I felt, as a mother too, the mixture of regret and sadness as you spoke of making more of the good times, especially when you didn't have health issues. This regret is so common in us mothers. Why didn't we do x, y, or z when we could? Why did we lose our temper or lose our focus? Why didn't we make more of the opportunities in easier times? It's easy to fall into these regrets, but at the same time we can remind each other that we don't know what is around the corner; it's impossible. Neither do we have knowledge of what's going to happen, nor the imperative to reach some ideal of perfection that we curate in our minds.

The longer we continue on our motherhood voyage, wading our way through high and low tides, the more we face the reality that we can only do our best with the circumstances we are in. And aiming for 'perfect', and then feeling disappointed when we sink, is something we collectively need to sail away from.

I've been looking for help with my challenges too, particularly on days I can't do the things I planned. As I look for strength through reading, I keep coming back to these following two *hadīth*s; the first filled with hope and the second with comfort, reassuring us that none of the hardship is empty or in vain:

Abū Mūsā al-Ashʿarī (ﷺ) reported: The Messenger of Allah (ﷺ) said, "When a slave of Allah suffers from illness or goes on a journey, he is credited with an equal reward of whatever good works he used to do when he was healthy or at home."[13]

And:

Abū Hurayrah (ﷺ) reported that: The Prophet (ﷺ) said: "Never is a believer afflicted with discomfort, illness, anxiety, grief or mental anguish, or even something as trivial as the pricking of a thorn, except that Allah will expiate his sins on account of his patience."[14]

We travel great distances in our mind, finding ourselves in unnamed places. Lost. With these two *ḥadīth*s, we find our way home.

Your post helped me sit with the subject of gratitude and really think about it. Years upon years of good health can easily lull us into forgetting that this isn't a guarantee we are entitled to – it is a privilege, a blessing. Other struggles occupy us, fog our mind, and we lose sight, forgetting the things to be grateful for. Thank you for reminding me, too, that real thankfulness to Allah, The Most Generous, manifests as consistent actions: daily acts of *ʿibādah*, helping others, giving *ṣadaqah* with whatever resources we have whether time, energy or donations.

As a mother, you understand the needs of your children best. Why is it that we, mothers, feel we're not enough? Please don't think they need anyone other than you. It's inevitable that on tough days, you wish the healthy, well version of yourself back and to cope the way you used to.

---

13 *Ṣaḥīḥ al-Bukhārī*: 2996
14 Agreed upon. *Ṣaḥīḥ al-Bukhārī*: 5641; *Ṣaḥīḥ Muslim*: 2572.

Allah's (ﷻ) plans can go over our head or take years to come to completion and make sense to us, but they are His designs. And I sense, from what you say, that the struggle is real. I don't doubt that for a minute, nobody can understand the struggles you have. But there's one thing I'm sure of, even as an outsider: you are the best mother for your children. What they gain from you is unique. In time, their storehouse of experience will be a life-force for someone else in this world.

We all need help along our mothering journey. And we all need different types of help. There's no shame in that. Some of us are fighting battles that no one will ever know about. We will need support to raise our children. That support could be practical and hands-on for one mother, for another it's a compassionate ear on a regular basis that keeps her going. I hope you've found help in practical and emotional ways to give you some succour and ease.

When I read about how you feel too deflated sometimes to make *du ʿāʾ*, it reminded me of the time when a Companion asked the Prophet (ﷺ) if he needed to whisper or call out loud when supplicating to Allah (ﷻ). The beautiful answer to this query came as direct revelation in this hopeful and healing *āyah*:

> [Prophet], if My servants ask you about Me, I am near. I respond to those who call Me, so let them respond to Me, and believe in Me, so that they may be guided.[15]

Knowing that we are never really ever alone, as this *āyah* confirms, is solace to our hearts when we feel isolated. In

15 *Sūrah al-Baqarah* 2:186.

those moments of despair, when there is no one else and we're on our knees with head and heart in submission, we are not alone – we are heard. Some days, I too have felt like 'what's the point?'. This *āyah* then turns into a lifejacket to stop me from drowning.

Thank you again for posting your experience that found me in my time of need.

With my *du'ā's* for your good health, ease and *barakah* for your family,

Love from your 'virtual' sister x

13

DEAR MOTHERS
STRUGGLING TO BE 'FAIR'

From:

Tasneem Jay

Grandparent,

Contributor to 'Heart Notes'

Sakina Family Magazine

Welcome, beloved readers, to a new section called Heart Notes!

I'm delighted to join the Sakina Family writers to share my experience of family life and those tricky situations no one prepares us for! Join the discussion and drop me a line at tasneemsheartnotes@sakina.com.

There's a gift shop that's survived in our town for over twenty years. I took my children there, and now I take my grandchildren too. It's grown and includes an eco-craft café in the extension. I'm as keen to go as my grandchildren are when there's a craft session or for special occasions to spend their gift money. There's always something new like the German handmade wooden puzzles, sustainable toys or science experiments. Mostly, my attention's caught by the children and their parents there. As this shop is so close to the popular castle and fortress, I see people from all over the place come through.

Over the years, there's a scene I see play out regularly. The only things that change are the parents and the ages of the children. Other than that, it's the same scene – the 'trying to be fair' drama I'll call it for it now.

Sometimes this is amusing, intriguing and bewildering to watch. Two siblings choose totally different items; one might pick the fidget spinner, the other reaches for the Pro Home Planetarium Kit. They are individuals and they know it! Last week, this scene played out again ...

The drama

Two brothers, probably three years apart were told the golden words by their mother 'now choose something you like', and so they lunged off to different display tables. The younger brother picked up four of the same pocket money toy; quantity clearly mattered to him, over quality, perhaps he was a collector.

The older brother, observing the younger brother's picks, looked like he was calculating which card to play after taking a quick look around the shop. Should he have a high decibel tantrum, or pick the 'it's not fair he's getting four of those' line? A tough decision. Instead he chose tactic number three: bargaining. He informed his mother that he'll forego the largest mechanical building set on the display table if and only if she promises to stop in the shop next door for the latest PS4 game. A good proposal, made smoothly, even walking a few steps away to give his mother time to think it through.

The elder delivered his bargain, while the younger relentlessly repeated how four of the same thing was exactly what he needed. The poor mother was flustered, embarrassed, clearly tired after the castle excursion and in need of a coffee. She negotiated until both children got two pocket money gadgets each. Neither boy looked happy and the mother by this stage no longer looked like she cared. She had been fair and equal after all, and isn't that the goal: equally fair, fairly the same?

An age-old problem

This scene plays out time and again in different ways; brothers and sisters, multiple siblings, mothers bringing their child and a friend (that can be trickier depending on the friend's expectations) to this gift shop. Each time, I see well-meaning parents caught in the 'fairness' test.

It's natural and as old as civilisation itself. Siblings will compare, some less and some more. It seems to be an inherited knowledge from generations past that the more the siblings, the less intense the everyday competition. Some elders vouch there's simply too much else going on in big families and the privileges are generally fewer for all in the first place. My grandparents said that, as did their grandparents before them.

Fair isn't identical

Being a grandparent myself, what I wish I could tell the parents I see in the shop is that fair doesn't need to look identical. You can fulfil their needs and interests without it 'looking' the same. As children, the earlier they learn this the better. Later on it gets more complicated.

Previous articles in this magazine have commented on sibling rivalry and how fairness between children, especially of different gender, is a central tenet of our faith. So I'm not going to repeat the clear evidence about that. In a nutshell, the bare minimum required of parents is to treat their children equally when it comes to their wellbeing, resources, education and parents' time and attention. That's a given and foundational.

As our children grow up however, 'fairness' will keep coming up in new and challenging ways. The days of making sure they have the same number of pizza slices, wash an equal quantity of dishes and have equal access to technology and games will soon evaporate. These raw, yet tangible, needs are all too soon replaced with comparisons about who was understood, forgiven or supported, for instance. How do parents equalise these? Before that stage comes, it's worth pondering over some of the following.

Rizq **is the key**

Talk as a family about what *rizq* means and that *al-Razzāq* has already decided what portion of the world will be ours. Children are capable of understanding, especially when it's taught in relation to their real world experiences. Start small and simple. For example, food is an easy one (read: chocolates, cookies and treats) as what has been allocated as part of their *rizq* won't pass them by. Likewise, no amount of trying to get to the front of the queue will guarantee those fries if it is not part of their *rizq*. Young teens upwards will raise good examples and explore new angles.

Take a positive view of your childrens' differences and encourage them to value their differences too. Not that one person is better or worse, but unique. Wouldn't the world be dull if all siblings were the same! They have a host of exclusive abilities, along with a range of distinctive challenges. So as parents, explain to them that it only makes sense that their needs are going to be met in different ways too. The sooner they see that different is not unfair, but 'bespoke', the better for everyone.

A note of caution too, let's not confuse the positive of 'individuality' with the harm of 'individualism'. A heavy subject you're thinking. Yes, it is. Individuality is about their personality and inherent nature. Individualism, on the other hand, is what our society is steeped in; that 'me, myself and I' culture. Sometimes we have to look critically at the messages we, the adults, are taking from those one-liners online. Individualism is the opposite of caring for one's family, neighbours and community. It gets confused with setting boundaries (which the Qur'ānic framework and Sunnah do already) and taking care of oneself.

Back to our children, as they get older, we manoeuvre in new ways to meet their needs and those altered steps look like we're not being 'equal'. But the deep well of dedication and love those steps are coming from is exactly the same. That's what our children need to understand.

Being a grandparent now, I can reflect on how I did things years back. At the time I didn't have the luxury of thinking it all through – I was on the go as you all are now! When I think back, I recall how I spent more energy and time on helping our eldest daughter work on the social relationships in her life. With the younger twin daughters, we put more effort into one twin's outdoor interests, while the other twin faced more educational struggles, so we supported her in ways her sisters never needed. Nothing was the same, even with the twins!

Speaking to those at the grandparent stage, who have jumped through so many parenting hoops, some still confess to being stumped with their adult childrens' sibling issues. Much of it comes back to that raw childhood 'fairness' subject. Left unchecked, comparisons can simmer away for decades, holding elderly parents to account for a catalogue of 'fair' or 'unfair' charges. This is the case when *rizq* isn't understood or only partially appreciated. There is only a certain amount of 'fairness' in a parent's hand, the rest is what Allah (ﷻ) has planned. And that plan was written before we came into being. If this understanding is firmly held on to, there would be a lot less friction within us.

So, with this thing called 'hindsight' I now have, I hope this month's 'Heart Note' brings some light and ease to your family life. I hope you have a beautiful spring break and look after your heart too while nurturing the ones around you. And if you find yourself in a gift shop, stressing to be 'fair', relax and treat yourself to a fidget spinner!

Your supporter & sister in building families,
Tasneem

14

DEAR MOTHER WHO'S FEELING AFRAID

From:
A fellow passenger observing you
A minoritized woman
A Mother wearing a symbol of faith
On public transport
Daily

Mama of two beautiful children,

We are on the same bus. I noticed you board with your young children and sit in the row in front of me. Just like that I had a flashback to the years I lugged the shopping and my little ones on to this bus too! My lot now drive their own cars and buy their meals, no need for public transport or me. Some friends find it funny, but I still like the long bus ride even after all these years. I get to see new shop fronts and these trendy delis and cafes popping up.

I stare out the window and carry on reminiscing. Watching you settle your children reminds me of those days, of whirling through the years. I could get lost in those memories, until the next stop brings me back to the present. We both look up at the same woman. It's funny how the atmosphere can shift so quickly from carefree to tense. It's a small place, a bus, at times like this.

A momentary glance is enough to see the expression set into the muscles of her face as she stomps past the driver. How do you describe it? Scornful, hateful, angry, in pain or hurt? Her steps, her arms, the tight fists of her hand, the clenched jaw, those searing eyes – and our antenna feels the danger. No mask either. It's bad enough we live in a world where some men pose a threat on public transport. But like you and I know, when someone is an identifiable Muslim woman, the aggression we face can come from women too. That's when the solidarity supposedly shared by women from all backgrounds doesn't work for us in the same way.

You look at the blissful oblivion of your eager son and daughter sitting beside you. They compare the plastic monsters that popped out of their Kinder eggs.

Your lioness senses rise to the fore, and you assess who's around you: behind across the aisle, three single women passengers are sat separately and right at the back sits a slight, wiry looking middle-aged man with headphones on. In front of you there's an elderly couple. The husband looks restless and uncomfortable. Every so often his wife places her hand on his.

How many of us mothers who stand out because of our skin colour or our hijab know this 'antenna' way of living? You know it. Being on guard. High alert. Ready to miss that bus or change seats or leave the train carriage if we detect a threat. Contingency get-out plans snap up within 15 seconds of spotting a possible risk. This is how we live. And we think this is normal? We know it's not normal. Even if we never say a word about it, we feel it. With two children by your side it's natural you're more vigilant than I am. You are a young mother, the matriarch, protecting her little ones.

You marvel at yourself; at how quickly you've assimilated all this information while you take a glance at your children again. Your neck feels warmer with a tinge of nerves sweeping over you. The scowling woman sits down towards the front. Relief; now you're sure she's not heading towards you. Relax now, enjoy this part of the route past the lake and the wildlife surrounding it. The poppies are the tallest I've seen this year.

'Mama look, my monster's got a red waistcoat ... and his one's got a green hat.'

You smile and nod back, not knowing what you're agreeing about. It could be a dinosaur, a chicken, a brick or a monster. It doesn't matter while your antenna is on high alert, anticipating and dreading some racial slur or anti-Muslim abuse.

You turn your face firmly away by looking left, out of the window, as though you're interested in the old high street we've turned on to. It's nothing like the new end of town. The quaint pastel green painted buildings are mostly vets and private surgeries now. At the same time your right eye is straining to see where the angry looking woman is heading after she stands up and starts walking in your direction. She's bumped into a teenage girl and scowls:

'Can't you get out the flipping way?!'

You were right. That maternal instinct, the sixth sense switched on for a good reason. In what feels like minutes but is only seconds, you sigh in relief as she's gone upstairs. A glance at the monitor confirms this as you see the back of her head move swiftly along the top deck.

Finally, you can relax. You let out another sigh and as you

glance briefly behind you, our eyes meet. We communicate without a sound. Aren't our eyes a miracle in the invisible language they speak!

'What was it you got in the shell, Sana?' you ask, genuinely relieved to go back to the trivia of childhood that won't be disturbed by a confrontation, abuse or worse. Those videos of Muslim women being abused on public transport have lodged themselves somewhere in our minds, haven't they? I try to forget them, but once you've seen it you can't 'unsee' it. It stays alive, reminding us that this does happen. It's not from thirty or forty years ago. It's here and now. I tell myself not to dwell on it, to focus on the good things, that most people are fine. But the image pops up at such tense moments.

How have we got to this stage of surveying our surround-ings like this?

The post office stop is always a long one, I suppose there's no other bus along this stretch. That once innocent letterbox! I never paid it any attention in the past, but now it's part of our story, isn't it? I suppose *that's* how we've ended up scanning people and places the way we do. When the politicians drop the odd remark – that's all it is for them – 'letterboxes'. Words so insignificant and every day, but used wrongly they can transform into a rod that's shared around the country by citizens who seek to punish us. And for what? For existing? That 'letterbox' label then ended up being strangely ironic as the global pandemic and mask wearing gave it a new meaning.

What is the root of the aggression we see on our screens?

The hijab pulled off on the bus, the young woman pushed at the edge of the train platform, the abuse hurled at that mother of three at the cash machine?

If only those of influence realised the consequence of the words they carelessly toss, like the men outside the café we've just passed tossing their cups in the bin. Those words become toxic droplets that seep into minds looking for someone to blame for their own misery. People who lash out at others don't do so from a place of contentment or happiness. There are usually long-term frustrations and problems festering. So, when public 'throwaway' comments are carried in the wind and fall on these fertile patches, they take root easily and spread like ivy. They keep the cycle of hate and ignorance growing, unstoppable and with stubborn roots.

There's no quick remedy for the fear you felt a few minutes ago. I recognise each of your moves. I understand why you're cautious and I also know how unhealthy it is to be like this, year on year. Who measures the stress caused by this way of living? All I can offer is my understanding, another mother who's walked the same cautious steps with the tender hands of her children clasped in hers. These little ones are oblivious to the real world, seeing their whole world in you while you shelter them.

Even though we might go through waves of internalising fear, and then rising above it, we need to keep in mind that our young children will experience the world the way we are, and take cues from us. It took me time to be mindful of the energy I was sending out to them and change this. They deserve to trust and embrace the overwhelming good in people. It takes some work and time though, I know. It takes even more work when 'we' are going through another round of being in the headlines.

I hope you stay safe and enjoy the simplicity of your little ones, today and always. Maybe I'll see you soon again on this route.

Yours,
Fellow Mother and passenger

15

DEAR MOTHER
IN THE GROCERY SHOP AISLE

From:
A Supermarket Assistant
In the Dairy aisle by day,
'Our Basket' Blog writer
by night.
Your local grocery

Blog post

When Halal reaches the Heart

She's been standing in this aisle for a good four minutes and twenty-two seconds while other shoppers have whizzed through here, returned for a forgotten item, and are now three aisles on. She's still here weighing up whether or not to buy that marinade and figuring out where to stand on the 'halal or not halal spectrum' of 'white wine vinegar'. In her other hand sits the non-frozen puff pastry with alcohol in it. She's pulled out her phone, searched it, and is now awkwardly scrolling through the results, basket balanced precariously on one arm.

In Ramadan some customers double their efforts in food label checking that are, to be fair, good enough for the other eleven months. But this month in particular, the teaching that *du'ā*'s are not being accepted for 40 days if something unlawful is eaten, seems to keep mothers doing more steps as they pace the aisles and search for ingredient information.

Feeding our families halal is a big deal. People don't always understand what mothers go through to make sure their family's not deliberately eating the wrong thing. It must count in the good deed checkout, it's well intentioned.

For this week's post, I'm going to take the subject of 'halal' food in a new direction. I'll leave the E numbers and types of gelatine for another post. Instead, I'll share what the elderly lady with the burnt orange blazer and ochre shawl said to me the other day as I was unpacking the kefir. We got talking when she asked me if we stock the latest kefir shots. Well, it only took a minute to go from that question to a comment about yoghurts, to frowning at the vanilla mousses on offer, and then she said:

'We all know the importance of eating halal, as in 'what is permitted', by going over the ingredients or having those endless debates about HMC or HFA and slaughter methods,' she put four small bottles of organic whole milk in her trolley and then carried on, 'but our community rarely talks about what's *ṭayyib* – do you know what that means?' Before I could think, she took a deep breath and told me anyway, '*ṭayyib* means what's wholesome, natural and sustainable. You know, grown without causing damage, pure. Instead of everyone being fixated on 'halal' – even though the 'halal' processed food is no good for anyone – we need to think about how food is grown.' She then reached over for a block of organic butter. 'Food that is wholesome is aligned to our *īmān* and behaviour. If you ever get the chance to look it up, you'll see the connections,' and she was off, disappeared before I could mutter a word.

That was the first time I heard halal food discussed like this. Not in all the years growing up do I remember anyone talking about 'ṭayyib' food. I got thinking about this, so that weekend I looked up online what halal and ṭayyib actually mean. The web took me all over the place: farming practices, food production systems, obesity being a global epidemic (the preventable sort), the link between physical and spiritual wellness. The meaning of the word ṭayyib extends to our intentions, income, food and drink – all being pure. Another common message I encountered from one site to the next was that highly processed foods and methods of food production that harm the earth can't be described as ṭayyib. That was no surprise, as all the artificial chemicals that go into processed foods are no good for us either.

Learning about this from the Sunnah, too, was more than a nudge for me, and that's why I'm sharing it, with 'Our Basket' readers. The noble Prophet (ﷺ) taught us about how our wellbeing and what we eat is balanced and linked to our behaviour. In contrast to how we behave as shoppers and a community, there's no emphasis on eating mountains of meat and poultry. While researching, what hit me was these verses from the Qur'ān that link eating what is pure and permissible to the basics of our faith: gratitude to Allah (ﷻ), our *īmān* (belief) and worship, and how God conscious we are. I'd never thought of it that way. Here's a few verses I found:

> *O you who have believed, eat from the good things which We have provided for you and be grateful to God if it is [indeed] Him that you worship.*[16]

---

16 *Sūrah al-Baqarah* 2:172.

Then eat of what God has provided for you [which is] lawful and good. And be grateful for the favour of God, if it is [indeed] Him that you worship.[17]

Oh, ye messengers! Eat of the good things (ṭayyibāt) and do righteous deeds. Surely, I know what you do.[18]

As with all 'Our Basket' posts I write, there's more than meets the eye. What started with the lady asking for kefir not only got me researching the difference between halal and *ṭayyib*, but it also made me think about how much effort goes into nourishing our hearts to keep our *īmān* healthy. We spend forever on satisfying taste buds and stomachs, way beyond our needs. If we were to balance our time looking for what keeps our *īmān* healthy, then we'll do ourselves a favour.

Imagine if we spent the same effort on looking at the ingredients of what our family watches online, what ideas they consume, what they drink in with their ears? All of this goes to the heart and affects us. We know what takes us closer to Allah (ﷻ), or further away from Him. If we're eating what's *ṭayyib*, or wholesome, and are careful about what goes into our hearts, our physical and mental health would improve greatly. The challenge is putting the same effort into both areas.

As we, mothers, are generally the ones who decide on what's bought in the grocery shop and then cooked; we have the opportunity to help our children and young people look at food in a better way. We can encourage thinking about

---

17 *Sūrah al-Naḥl* 16: 114.
18 *Sūrah al-Anbiyāʿ* 23: 51.

how pure the food is and make better choices about cooking something from scratch rather than buying the processed version. We can show them that food choices aren't just about finding the green halal label, but thinking about what our body needs in the right quantity.

Step by step, we can show the links made in the Qur'ān between eating from what's pure and our worship and values that please Allah (ﷻ). Without this approach, we're making it harder for our children to face the challenges and get over the hurdles they will face. Nutrition of their *īmān* and body should help in some way, to tackle the complicated world we live in.

The mum holding the frozen pastry pack and reading some random person's post on a forum about alcohol in food is still standing there, sifting through the search results. I wonder what's going through her head as she scrolls through link after link. She's put the marinade back on the shelf – it had too many preservatives anyway. And the pastry? That must be fine as she's finally dropped it in her basket.

Till my next post dear Mothers, I hope we all find the ways and means for a *ṭayyib* way of living – nurturing our body, soul and the beautiful earth that feeds us.

Your sister @OurBasket

16

DEAR MOTHER
WHO IS DEPLETED FROM GIVING

From:
My Daily Journal
Late night, mid-week
At any stage of mothering

Today is one of those days – I caught a glimpse of your jaded eyes when I rushed through the hall to make it out on time. I admit I barely recognised you.

I heard your voice this morning. It weighed heavy, drawn and reluctant; constricted throat muscles to hold back the tears. Some days are more of a struggle than others for no obvious reason, nothing out of the ordinary happened today. So why is every interaction and routine overwhelming?

What's going on? The hours come and go as they normally do, calling on you to fulfil the needs of your family. You morph as you always do; rising and falling, stepping and leaping, lunging and pulling back as the needs require, as the hands of the clock choreograph every cell in your body to keep going and giving.

You don't like to think of it as 'giving' as that wouldn't be very noble of you. Your inner voice reminds you that to think like that might even be selfish. But you continue to give of yourself, as that's what you do.

On good days, your energy and ability to handle your family's needs seems to flow from an endless well – a well that is buoyed up with the natural instinct of what a mother does. And you don't question your flow of energy, in fact you embrace it.

All those conversations with friends and family, and those instructive Islamic books you've read, live in the backroom of your mind. The soundbites continue to echo as you haul the second load of laundry up each step of the stairs and around a tight corner. *You're honoured to be a mother. You are blessed. Motherhood is the highest station.* These phrases carry your footsteps as though you're ascending a podium of honour. And by the time you make it to the top of the stairs and drop the basket down, thoughts of gratitude resonate within you. *It's true,* you scold yourself, *how many others do I know longing for that small person to crawl on to their lap, cling to their legs, spill their blackcurrant juice on their sage cotton top? How many women are desperate to smell the foreheads of their sleepy child in the nape of their neck?*

It's with this reminder of the status, honour and blessing that you approach the fourth nappy change of the day with a subconscious prayer that THIS one will, along with the others, count on the scale of reward. Lower back stiffening, you exhale another *du'ā'* for all this to be recorded as *'ibādah* – a worship. Your mind is two steps ahead, noting that another feed is due for however long it takes for mouthfuls of you to quench her thirst.

The wet laundry is asking for a warm place to stretch out and regain its paler shade, the hoover in the hall and breakfast bowls in the kitchen wait in the queue expectantly. As long as you get it done before the afternoon pick up; that's the minimum you need to do, to reach neutral, from where you can think about the day ahead.

On this good day, you can handle this, even embrace it because you know that this work of mothering is an honour.

You know this work of establishing a family is a sacred struggle. You know mothers give, so you do it willingly.

Today is not a good day though. Today, giving and appreciating the role are at war with one another. The appreciative, grateful you, ready and willing to shoulder this role is at odds with the mentally, emotionally, spiritually depleted you.

Today giving grates. It grazes your soul, makes you gasp like experiencing a cold water shock, stings like a wedge of lemon plastered on an ulcer in your cheek. You don't feel like giving, but you need to.

Yes, that word 'need' takes centre stage. You need to chop those vegetables, you need to wash their clothes and pick up the hurricane they left in the bathroom and you need to still be 'nice'. That bit can be the hardest need on a day like this: being 'nice'. That soulless word that's expected of good mothers. 'Nice' doesn't work today as you can't see or feel what 'nice' looks like. Today there's no logical reason for the resistance you feel in serving others around you.

So you give and give.
You give from your bones
You give from your mind
You give from your fingertips
You give from your heart
You give from your eyes and ears
You give from your lungs
You give from your spine

You give because, you remind yourself, they are the children, you are the adult and they need you. And besides, is there any other option today, in this hour of their need, other than to serve? You debate with yourself: *if I didn't need help yesterday, then why am I struggling with exactly the same things today?* You know the answer and it deserves attention. Like other mothers you've become too good at ignoring the signs of depletion.

How are you going to move past this?

Step back just for a few moments and float above; away from your home, your routine and children, and some realities will come into sharper focus. Do you see it now? Do you see that this amount of giving isn't supposed to be done alone? That your expectations on yourself, on your shared parenthood, are too wide and vast to be accomplished by one person?

> There's a good reason that communities have multiple adults raising children – but today's nuclear family lifestyle is taking its toll on mothers the most. It's up to us to make the change. We need to create their circle of support to bring balance back into their life. It's urgent and well overdue.

The woman on that talk show had a point. Since you've met a couple of new parents through the nursery, a quick chat or sharing notes is helpful. Wasn't this how your foremothers coped with the demands of family life: as part of a community? They didn't accept burn-out as a natural consequence of mothering. Tired and challenged, yes. And that reminds you of the verses which bring hope and peace:

So, truly with every difficulty, there is relief,
Truly with every difficulty there is relief.
Therefore, when you are free from your immediate task,
still labour hard,
And to your Sustainer turn all your attention.[19]

And:

God desires ease for you, He does not desire hardship from
you...[20]

You know from years of listening to other women speaking, there is one common thread they all hold when the feeling same way as you do today: they've neglected their inner and outer selves. You spend so much time trying to understand the needs of your immediate family, you no longer know yourself. *What do I need? What can I do differently before reaching this point?* And it's only when you start asking yourself these questions and make small changes, that you prevent reaching this stage that I call 'giving depletion'.

For today, acknowledge and accept the burn-out for what it is. It is not failure, it's a temporary empty tank; a parched plant that needs feeding. This day isn't defining you. Your children will not suffer from getting less of you for a day or two or more. You know how much they receive from you every day, year on year.

If you need the shortest route to get beyond feeling burn-out, remember these signposts:

The first is to remember it is a noble service to look after yourself, and to give to yourself too. Giving ourselves

---

19 *Sūrah al-Sharḥ* 94: 5-8.
20 *Sūrah al-Baqarah* 2: 183.

spiritual nourishment, physical outlets and mental and emotional space are essential. Meet these needs and feel strengthened.

Secondly, remember that all your work – stepping in and stepping back, your presence or deliberate absence, your constant chameleon-like changing colour to compliment new spaces that bloom in your family's lives – is seen and recorded by *al-Khabīr*, The All-Aware.

You know your role is honoured and rewarded fairly in both worlds. It's easy to forget this because the scales people use to measure life are complicated. *What do you do to earn a living? So when are you going back to work? Haven't you heard of childcare? I wouldn't do all that, it's not your job.* and on and on. Each voice comes up with a different set of measures and this adds to the mental exhaustion you're feeling. All those ideas about what a mother should or shouldn't be doing flying around in your head. By all these worldly scales your effort won't always be counted, and this can leave you feeling devalued and invisible. Our Sustainer sees and hears all, and none of your efforts today are going to waste.

And the last signpost is to stay close to the best companion when the journey feels uncertain: gratitude. Staying close to this companion will bring some peace and contentment for what you do have: your health, your family, your sustenance and your *īmān*. On a good day you're well aware of all this and more. But like everyone else, you can forget too.

A better day is there on the other side of this page.

With love from,
Yourself

17

DEAR MOTHERS CONNECT TO NATURE!

From:
Shaheen Malik
Scout Group Leader
Mother & grandmother
Hilal Scouts Group

As-salāmu ʿalaykum!

It was wonderful to welcome the Scouts back for the summer sessions. They were bursting with energy and enthusiasm, eager to dive into new challenges. We look forward to developing their skills this term with some amazing opportunities *in shāʾ Allāh*.

This month, I'm delighted to share the newsletter with a difference. Alongside the updates, one Hilal Scout Group volunteer will write a personal letter to you on a topic of her or his choice. So here goes, I'm first up with a subject at the centre of my heart: our connection to nature.

What I hear ...

It's been the hugest adventure to lead the unit over the past five years and learn from young people in the process. One of the things I've observed spending time with them is their experience of the natural environment. Our young people are good at sharing their views, and what I hear from them is that the majority feel disconnected to their natural surroundings.

They expressed something unexpected: that they see activities in the natural environmental as something 'specialists' need to lead, or if it's 'green issues', it's seen as something only activists are concerned about! I was intrigued. It's true that climate change and sustainability are complex issues, overwhelming us all at some point. Thinking over their views, I could see how they've come to look at the natural environment as a place for people in hiking gear on a mission to protect a dying tree species, or only accessible if you're part of a group like The Ramblers. They're not seeing enough people like themselves involved with our natural environment. So, to counter this, I believe it's all the more vital we revive the benefits of being outside in nature for us all!

From the Cubs up to the Explorers, we see how much your children gain from being outdoors, quite besides the activity we're focusing on. The time we spend with them in Scouts is very little, so I'm sharing five reflections, based on my personal experience, in the hope this benefits the whole family.

1. The Qur'ānic viewpoint

Yes, that's right, the natural environment is mentioned countless times for many purposes in the Glorious Qur'ān. After all, Allah (ﷻ) is *al-Muṣawwir* – The Shaper, *al-Mubdi'* – The Initiator, *al-Bādī* – The Originator, and *al-Khāliq*, The Creator of all, grand or minute. Natural phenomena are called 'āyāt', they are His signs that strengthen our *īmān* and teach us:

And it is He who spread the Earth and made in it firm mountains and rivers, and of all fruits, he has made in it two kinds; He makes the night cover the day; most surely there are signs in this for a people who reflect.[21]

He causes to grow for you thereby herbage, and the olives, and the palm trees, and the grapes, and of all the fruits; most surely there is a sign in this for a people who reflect.[22]

These are two out of so many more *āyāt*. We are clearly tasked with being the earth's 'caretakers', or *khalīfah*s. We're expected to care about the welfare of every living creature and resource around us. The Qur'ān draws our attention to so many issues about this planet we inhabit; reminding us not to waste, to be grateful, warning us about the effects of destroying these assets. We're advised to tread on the earth carefully and mindfully:

The servants of the Lord of Mercy are those who walk humbly on the earth, and who, when ignorant people address they say words of peace.[23]

When our *dīn* is infused with an appreciation of the signs of the Creator, how can we remain detached from it? Even in our little town, the sheer miracle of nature is all around us, right on our doorstep. Every path through the valley of Ridge Woods within reach of all our families, is packed with different plants and trees. Only a couple of months ago the bluebell and crocuses carpet were astounding, *subḥān Allāh*.

---

21 *Sūrah al-Raʿd* 13: 3.
22 *Sūrah al-Naḥl* 16: 11.
23 *Sūrah al-Furqān* 25: 63.

2. Our history

It's no surprise that the history of Muslim civilisation includes a huge amount of scholarship and design related to the environment. It's from the hands of Muslim scholars that volumes were written in the eighth century onwards examining air and water pollution, waste disposal and public health and about protecting wildlife and ecosystems. Some of our Scouts will remember a short film we watched about this. It would make a great family project to find out more over the summer holidays.

Scholars from Damascus, Tunisia, Egypt and Iraq, amongst others, wrote about our relationship to the environment. Whether this was about air quality in markets and buildings or the use of water use in public spaces. Environmental development across Muslim civilisation took the shape of underground networks of aqueducts known as *qanawāt*, water purification systems, water powered mills and much more.[24]

There were works on animal rights in the market detailing how the '*Muḥtasib*' – the market inspector – would check if water fountains and bread stations were functioning properly for stray cats and dogs. Likewise, laws were passed about animal welfare. 17th century Ottoman decrees prohibited overloading working animals and making sure they had Friday as a rest day each week.

24 https://muslimheritage.com/1000-years-amnesia-environ-ment-tradition-in-muslim-heritage/

Authors of that time took a holistic approach, aligning environmental issues to the health of the mind and body. Some literature went further to explore the impact of the natural surroundings on the heart and soul of a person.

I was fascinated to discover that connecting to the natural surroundings was prescribed to help certain emotional states, alongside keeping good company, and taking up new activities. 'There are nine properties in the soul', Ibn Sīnā wrote in the preface to his poem on medicine, *al-Urjūzah fī'l-Ṭibb*, 'Five of them are related: hearing, sight, smell, taste and touch in its entirety: one goes to the nerves, through it one moves his joints; another represents objects as seen through a mirror; another governs thought; the last memory.'[25] By this he foregrounded the numerous ways the outer affects the inner. So, when we look at it like this, a stroll in all those acres of parkland to the east of our town would be considered a treatment. What are we waiting for!

3. Contemplating the signs in nature

How amazing is it, that contemplating nature is part of our *'ibādah*! This was my lifeline when our children were young, and has continued to be the most grounding, peaceful way to spend time outside. Reflecting on what we see around us increases our love and awe for Our Creator and humility towards this Earth He has entrusted to us.

---

25 *Avicenna's Poem on medicine*, Ibn Sina, *Al-Urjuzah Fi Al-Tibb: Avicenna's Poem on Medicine*, ed and trans by Haven C. Krueger Springer, 1963 pp. 20-21

And He has subjected to you, as [a gift] from Himself, all that is in the heavens and on the earth. Behold, in that are signs indeed for those who reflect.[26]

Children are naturally inclined to the outdoors. When we can gently align their love of the beauty, patterns, textures and features in the trees, the wildflowers, even the shape of the clouds, to appreciating the Creator's magnificence, they are then engaged in contemplating as a part of daily life. Remember, it doesn't have to be grand botanical gardens! The evergreens we walk past daily, the clusters of forget-me-not on the roadside, the reeds along the stream that flows through our town and all the life in the stream are freely available to us all.

The benefit to our heart and soul of reflecting on the elements, whether young or old, is multiple. Looking back at history again, we see contemplating on nature was built into the design of the Islamic gardens and courtyards which spread across Muslim civilisation, making this connection an *īmān* boosting part of daily life.

These powerful translated *āyāt* give me no end of inspiration to step outside! Remember, stargazing is part of contemplating the stunning natural world we live in.

Indeed, in the creation of the heavens and the earth and the alternation of the day and night there are signs for people of reason. They are those who remember Allah while standing, sitting, and lying on their sides, and reflect on the creation of the heavens and the earth and pray, "Our Lord! You have not created all of this without purpose. Glory be to You!

26 *Sūrah al-Jāthiyah* 45: 13.

Protect us from the torment of the Fire.[27]

Do you not see that Allah sends down rain from the sky, and We produce thereby fruits of varying colours? And in the mountains are tracts, white and red of varying shades and [some] extremely black.[28]

And He has made subservient for you the night and the day and the sun and the moon, and the stars are made subservient by His commandment; most surely there are signs in this for a people who ponder.[29]

It is He who shows you the lightening by way of fear and hope. It is He Who raises up the clouds, heavy with fertilising rain. Thunder repeats His praise and so do the angels with awe ...[30]

4. Our grandparents – sustainability trailblazers!

We hear complex things about threats to our environment in the news such as climate change, biodiversity loss and air and water pollution amongst much else. I know it can get overwhelming. In our everyday life though, we can make the *niyyah* (intention) in our hearts not to add further damage to our planet through our hands.

Not wasting food or household items, mending and using what is locally available were a way of life for our grandparents' generation. It wasn't one special month, or

27 *Sūrah Āl ʿImrān* 3: 190-191.
28 *Sūrah Fāṭir* 35: 27-28.
29 *Sūrah al-Naḥl* 16: 12.
30 *Sūrah al-Raʿd* 13: 12-13.

day in the year when they made an effort. Their daily habits included using up perishables to cook and walking to local markets for what was in season. They made sure every part of a fruit or vegetable was used or preserved for longevity. We have a sweet activity this summer for the Scouts to make preserves from some local produce – keep your eyes peeled for that one! We may have less time now to do all these things, but one small change consistently can make a difference.

Our foremothers expertly reused fabrics, making quilts and soft furnishings, rather than throwing out good items. They did this out of a sense of accountability for the *amānah* put in their hands. There's a great message we can take from their way of living responsibly and honouring the resources around them.

Some of the creative upcycling can be valuable shared time together and a much needed alternative to screens and technology. After all these years of raising a family, I've found the best solutions to issues are often found in simple things, right there in front of us.

5. Step out to simplicity

Being outside is the destination – near or far. The sky will always have something to offer; be it feathered wings against the dramatic light and shadow display or the way the rainclouds disperse. Be conscious of the air – either a soft breeze lilting through branches, chilling gales or something in between. Wherever we live, a few minutes' walk takes us to a cluster of trees, a small park, or a recreation field.

Something about being outdoors helps all of us emotionally too, diffusing tensions on some days (yes, it happens to us all), and easing communication with our children when we feel demotivated. There is something that captures our souls, be it the open skies, the endless colours and shades around us, the textures, or the earth's musk after rainfall. It's the simplicity.

As always, I look forward to hearing your thoughts and about this. Send any nature pictures to us when you're out and about which inspire your family, and we'll share them in the next newsletter.

I hope these summer months will bring your family haystacks of happiness outdoors!

Shaheen Malik,
Scout Group Leader

18

DEAR MOTHER APPROACHING HER CHILD'S QUR'ĀN KHATM

From:
Ustādhah Khadijah
Qur'ān Teacher,
Local masjids
Madrasahs
All around the world

*And We reveal of the Qur'ān that which
is a healing and a mercy to the believers.*[31]

As-salāmu 'alaykum wa-raḥmatullāhi wa-barakātuh,

It gives me so much joy and gratitude to send you this letter. Each time one of my students finishes their first reading of the Qur'ān, I send this letter to the special adult who supported them through this noble journey – a journey unlike any other.

Together, bound by our love for the words of Allah (﷾), your child has reached this milestone. As much as we are grateful to the teachers and celebrate with the students, your investment – prioritising time for their reading and practice – is not forgotten by any of us.

Your child is now part of the global community reading the *Kitāb Allāh*. Today is a fitting time to remember just how significant this achievement is with the poignant sayings commending those who read and recite the Qur'ān:

31 *Sūrah al Isrā* 17:82

A person well-versed in reading the Qur'ān is equal in rank to the Noble, Pious, Scribes (angels who record all deeds). He who finds difficulty in reciting the Qur'ān will obtain two rewards.[32]

And:

> It was narrated that Abū Umāmah al-Bāhilī said: "I heard the Messenger of Allah (ﷺ) say, 'Recite the Qur'ān, for it will come on the Day of Resurrection to intercede for its companions. Recite the two bright ones, *al-Baqarah* and *Āl 'Imrān*, for they will come on the Day of Resurrection like two clouds or two shades or two flocks of birds in ranks, pleading for those who recite them. Recite *Sūrah al-Baqarah* for to take recourse to it is a blessing and to give it up is a cause of grief, and those engaged in witchcraft cannot confront it.'"[33]

Although there is no authentic tradition in the Sunnah that completing the reading is celebrated, nor is the celebration considered an obligation or act of worship in any way, there exists a spectrum of ways our ummah shows gratitude. These include feeding the needy, giving *ṣadaqah* (charity), rewarding our children with a gift and donating to the madrasah or institution where they learnt.

Around the world, from sprawling towns to the humble dwellings in rural communities, there are beautiful traditions that keep children encouraged in a circle of reciting; joining the millions before them and those around them. As long

---

32 *Ṣaḥīḥ Bukhārī* Bukhari and *Ṣaḥīḥ Muslim*.
33 *Ṣaḥīḥ Muslim*.

as we make sure our intention is to encourage the children, without excessive show (*riyā'*), then we hope marking this special milestone will become a treasured memory for your family.

We would like to invite you on a trip around the globe for a look at how they mark this occasion. In Somali nomadic traditions, for example, the family of the child being celebrated sacrifices an animal and shares the meat with the needy, relatives and friends. They gather together for a feast, inviting the child's teacher and showing gratitude for this huge achievement by giving gifts; traditionally new clothes for the student, and money to the teacher.

Whether it's called a *'khatame'* or *'Khatmī'*, the sense of joy to become fluent in reading the Qur'ān is the common thread that unites us all. In Nigeria, the celebration is called a *'walīmat al-Qur'ān'*. One of our teachers, Ustādhah Aminat, shared her memory:

> We call it *Wolimo* – a big celebration with fanfare for us in western Nigeria. *Yorubas* – we are the life and soul of celebrations!
>
> Students at madrasah will have been practising for the performance and graduates would have practised for months to read just *al-Fātiḥah* and the first five verses of *al-Baqarah*. All extended families and friends will be invited!
>
> On the day, there will be a programme of events: usually, *du'ā's* and lectures by imams on the importance of the Qur'ān. Then each child will be called to recite different portions of the Qur'ān to

show what they know. Afterwards parents come and show their happiness with songs and gifting money and prayers of *barakah* for the child. Once all children have finished, they will present them certificates of completion of the Qur'ān. These blessed gatherings are where there is recitation of the Qur'ān, *ṣalawāt* on the Prophet (ﷺ), *dhikr*, gratitude and *du'ā*'s for guidance. Our *du'ā* for your child now is that the Qur'ān remains the spring and light of her or his heart.

For some of our children, when they finish this first reading it introduces them to a lifelong path of becoming a *Ḥāfiẓ* or *Ḥāfiẓah*. Even for those of our children who don't follow the *ḥāfiẓ* path, it lifts our hearts and *īmān* to remember the position of our *ḥifẓ* students and their parents. What a blessed station they hold:

> It was narrated that Abū Hurayrah (ؓ) said: "The Messenger of Allah (ﷺ) said: 'The Qur'ān will come on the Day of Resurrection in the form of a pale man saying to its companion, 'Do you recognize me? I am the one who made you stay up at night and made you thirsty during the day...' Then he will be given dominion in his right hand and eternity in his left, and a crown of dignity will be placed upon his head, and his parents will be clothed with garments which far surpass everything to be found in this world. They will say, 'O Lord, how did we earn this.' It will be said to them, 'Because you taught your child the Qur'ān.'"[34]

---

34 *Ṭabrānī*.

It was narrated from 'Ā'ishah (☺) that the Prophet (☺) said: "The one who recites the Qur'ān and learns it by heart, will be with the noble righteous scribes (in Heaven) and the one who exerts himself to learn the Qur'ān by heart and finds it difficult, will have two rewards."[35]

Coming back to you, dear mother – your contribution is celebrated today too. You persisted to make the Qur'ān a central part of your child's life. When your child didn't want to attend, as all children do at some point, you were patient in guiding them. When you had more demands on your time than hours in the day, you prioritised your child's recitation practice. When a hundred types of entertainment could have filled their time, you consistently chose to be present with your child, to encourage their reading and practice.

Everyone learns to read and recite, you may be thinking to yourself, but it is quite the contrary. This is the best gift you could have planted in the heart of your children, and now I pray it will grow stronger and firmer each day. There is now a lifetime ahead of them to understand this communication from Allah (☺) to themselves, to answer their minds' questions, to have clarity about their purpose, to benefit their hearts and souls in the Qur'ān's *shifā'* (healing). As you and I know, the relationship with the Qur'ān goes far beyond perfecting the letters and sounds. It is the map for every area of our lives; moral, legal, physical, spiritual and emotional.

May our student, your child, have this relationship nurtured with love and gentleness so it's a life-long support.

35 *Bukhārī*.

In this Qur'ān We have put forward all kinds of illustrations for people, so that they may heed an Arabic Qur'ān, free from any distortion – so that people may be mindful.[36]

Ustādhah Khadijah

19

Dear Mother
LIVING WITH DOMESTIC ABUSE

From:
Erna
Fellow student
Languages Dept.
International Study Centre

Hi Huda,

Thank you for the email – this college account is useful after all. Yes, I've been worried about you and was relieved to hear from you. It's reassuring every time you turn up to the course, but for the past couple of weeks I wondered where you'd gone. There's no need to apologise about not receiving any texts or messages. I understand. From our half-finished conversations between seminars, it sounds like things are getting harder.

How can I help?

I've been thinking about your situation for days so I'm sharing some thoughts here. Huda, I hope you don't feel ashamed about this. Unfortunately, it is too common a problem and there is no community that can say they are immune from the scourge of domestic abuse and violence. Our conversations are so brief I've never got round to telling you my mother was in a similar situation to you when my brother and I were children. From a child's perspective, I've been through something similar to what you've described. We went through the experience of my mother taking us to escape for our safety. I know every situation is different, but I feel for you and your children. Decades have passed, our lives moved on for the better, but some emotions are never forgotten.

When you gave your free and joyful consent at your *nikāḥ*, the abuse you suffer today was the last thing you could have imagined. Ever. This was the furthest thing on your mind. This is what happens to *other* women, people imagine; the weak ones, forced into the *nikāḥ*, coerced to stay in the marriage, probably with less education, less choice, less voice. That's what people think, isn't it? How wrong these stereotypes are!

Today we've learnt the harsh truth that abuse does not fall on the shoulders of the weakest alone. It can fall on anyone's shoulders. In your case, you mentioned it came after the first few years of a peaceful marriage and two children. Circumstances changed, his behaviour deteriorated, temperaments altered and bit by bit, before you could recognise the abuse for what it was, you were gripped and consumed by it. How many women feel they're the only ones going through this, and have no place in their community if their struggles were to be known? The fear of being judged harshly and left as a pariah by the very people who should support vulnerable women and children is still pervasive. And so, the silence is pervasive too.

Abuse, as we started talking about that day, comes from psychological control, denigration, chipping away at your existence until there is little left of the person you were. And the abuse is not just 'domestic' as is easily misunderstood. From what you told me, the control started physically *outside* of your home; tracking your movements, where you worked, in all your communication with family and friends, in the financial sanctions to stifle any independence. The strategy worked as your world shrunk bit by bit.

Now that you've realised the way you're living is unacceptable, and recognised it as abnormal, you've taken the first step towards seeking help. Maybe even seeking help for him – because *some* do change. If caught at the right time, like a disease, this illness can be treated. If getting him help isn't an option right now (it doesn't sound like it is), then for the sake of yourself and your children, living in fear is not the way forward.

Living in fear is not the premise of a marriage – that sacred institution entered in the name of God. The only contract made between two people in His name to a life of mutual compassion, love, respect and protection. How easily do we as communities (our cultures are different, but the same problem exists) forget the purpose and spiritual union of the wedding? It gets washed away like the petals on the path.

If we take a step back and think about what it was all for, it might help to get some clarity.

The *libās* metaphor – '*they are your garments and you are their garments*' – is what a marriage should give us in our daily lives rather than a temporary appearance as a quote on wedding cards – where it is reduced to a momentary reminder and then easily forgotten.[37] Marriage is the clothing of compassion and protection first; it beautifies, it strengthens, it hides faults. God is beautiful and loves beauty. And this contract He has blessed is a source of

---

37 *Sūrah al-Baqarah* 2:187

protection, security and mercy.

Anyone suffering abuse can often try to rationalise their partner acting against these values – excuses for why she hides her achievements, excuses for why she doesn't want to be seen with a friend. But, dear Huda, the problem is that, when women do this, without realising it, they're replacing love and protection with fear and insecurity. Nobody sets out to say this, and deep down, no one believes this. Everyone knows this is not marriage.

You know what is right deep within you, it's finding the strength to act on what you know. It takes a huge amount of courage to imagine a future beyond this control and to replace the anxiety and panic with the security and comfort you and your children deserve.

In your email you described your worry about leaving the abuse. I'm copying that bit here as you mentioned you're deleting your inbox regularly:

> Most days I can't think straight, I'm writing to you from the library, (and getting here was a mission). Every time I think about taking a step, I abandon those thoughts. Honestly, talking to you is one thing, but thinking of doing anything is so hard. I know I need to if I want to save our lives from this misery. It's just so difficult.

> You're right, Erna, I don't know how you understood so quickly – yes I'm stuck in the narratives and excuses for him which got me through these years. But I'll admit, one by one, those excuses are falling away. I know the end of the line is close. It's getting worse.

I can't see how I can do it. How am I supposed to get up and leave? Like when? How does anyone do this, like in the middle of the night? How do I get my kids out without him noticing? Thinking of it puts me in an anxious freeze. The kids are his world. He says that he lives for them. He's usually good to them – it's us that don't get on, it's me he's got the problem with. It's taken so much to get to this class and now that would be lost too, if I ... I don't think I can rock the boat by changing anything at the moment.

I realise Huda, that there's a lot at stake with taking any action. You need support and I'm here to do whatever I can to help you. You've mentioned that your parents are understanding and wouldn't turn their back on you and your children, but they don't know the full situation. I'm sure when they do, they'll want your safety above anything else.

Maybe the first step is to think about what the future looks like if you stay? Our thoughts are powerful, and as you've said to me in class soon after the last incident, you know you need to leave for your safety.

It is a battle to think straight, I understand it. My mother only saved us and herself when she could turn a corner in her head and decide that leaving the restrictive, damaging thoughts was a way to save her life. She had to break free from those thoughts first. For one reason or another when women are controlled and in fear, it's easier to spin threads and build strong cocoons – we perceive these as protection around us and our minds continue to add layers. But if the threads are spun from a spool of oppression, we need to let these go and rebuild with new material. Thank God for a neighbour, a strong lady who was also a foster mother to many children, who knew what to do. She helped my mother think and take action.

When we spoke about the way taking actions looks different, in every situation, it's true. For some people, the first step is recognising things are not right; that first outburst, the signals. At this point, their action could be to find the help and support that will change things for the couple; rewiring the behaviours that have crept in at an early stage.

Many couples realise there are historic issues to heal from. They are parts of themselves that are broken and need addressing in order to improve the relationship with their spouse. Marriages and families are saved through professional help that comes early enough. And so too, along the spectrum, are measures women desperately need to take for the safety and protection of themselves and their children.

There should be no shame in seeking help. You're not alone going through this awful situation. As I read in an article recently, '1,300,000 women in England and Wales and an estimated ten million people at least in USA' are suffering violence at the hands of the person who is their partner.[38] I say 'person' as men can suffer too, albeit in fewer numbers.

Why is it that we as communities of believers become

---

38 685,000 male victims ONS figures 2018; *"National Statistics"*. NCADV.
   National Coalition Against Domestic Violence. Retrieved 5 October 2018.

fearful and embarrassed to broach this subject? We have no shame to research every resource and leave no stone unturned when looking for schools, or housing, or a doctor's surgery or a million other things. Then why do we neglect our own souls? Our minds, health and wellbeing have the same right to our time and efforts.

I remember a time when a student at the college I was teaching in, back in my country, showed me her bruises. I'd use every moment of that tea break to find who she could go to for her and her son's safety. Like so many mothers suffering the same situation, she was reluctant to think about any of the suggestions I was making to contact her relatives in a distant town. I realised it was complicated; that those relatives of her husband who could have intervened to protect her actually supported his brutal behaviour, making it all the more gut wrenching.

During that tea break (which I never realised would be the last one, as she left the course thereafter), I tried my best to emphasise one thing: there are options, there are ways to save herself and her child, ways to get some space to think about her situation and the threat she was under. All the time I spoke, I could see she understood and agreed, but taking a step ... that was too much.

So, I came from another angle: Islam doesn't allow this, I sounded desperate too, because I was. 'Your *dīn*, our faith, it doesn't allow you to suffer this. Staying in this danger isn't *ṣabr* – this isn't the type of patience asked of us. You have guardians who can protect you in the short term, please, for the sake of your child, go somewhere while you can.'

When I returned the following week with numbers and an address, I learnt she had left. We didn't have so many ways of contacting people in those days – just basic mobiles. Her number changed. I hope I can forgive myself one day for not getting help to her fast enough. One of the problems was that she found it difficult to accept her situation was not going to improve if she just kept quiet. It was that hope she clung to which stopped her taking up practical help.

So, Huda, when I see and hear someone in distress now, I take action. I write to you in the hope of helping in any way I can. At the very least I hope this will start the most important conversation you need to have, and that is with yourself. You have courage deep down, you have an intelligent mind, you have a strong heart to choose what is best for you all, for your protection and for a better future.

I'm here to help you and I've put a couple of numbers below for practical advice. Please stay in touch.

With love,
Erna

20

DEAR MOTHER
WHO NEEDS TO RECHARGE HER SPIRITUAL BATTERY

From:
The Editor
Soulfulmama.org
Editorial: An open letter to mothers
Issue no 2: volume 11

As-salāmu ʿalaykum,

Greetings of peace to you dearest readers.

I knew things weren't right when that feeling of emptiness infused daily life, along with a restlessness I couldn't explain. 'Life' itself felt like the wrong fit. Daily *ʿibādah* became mechanical, moving limbs disconnected to the heart, thoughts scattered like spilt peppercorns. Were these feelings the result of neglecting my spiritual needs, of putting everything else first before nourishing my soul?

Random past memories pop up when we least expect them. When I was feeling like this, a scene from my teenage years surfaced in my thoughts. There was a sticker I held onto for the longest time, stuck on the bottom right-hand corner of my notice board. From there, it was transferred to inside the cover of a diary where it lived for years until it frayed and faded. The words never faded, though. They remained a permanent light in my mind, guiding those formative years. The sticker read:

Everyone starts his day and is a vendor of his soul, either freeing it or bringing about its ruin.[39]

---

39 *Ṣaḥīḥ Muslim.*

These words of our beloved *Rasūl Allāh* (ﷺ) grew with me through all the peaks and troughs of becoming an adult. Was I freeing my soul through feeding it, or ignoring it and bringing its downfall? What choices had I made that day that aligned my soul with good traits, that increased its focus on the Hereafter? I'd ask myself these questions in the privacy of my diaries. This *ḥadīth* became the weighing scale for my time. Decades later, I've seen new sides to these deeply instructive words. I still need to realign myself when my spiritual battery is running low. I'm certain we all struggle in our own ways with keeping spiritually healthy, and so I decided to dedicate this issue to going back to the basics: how are we investing in our souls?

Motherhood is spiritual work. We're cultivating our children's hearts, minds and souls through their innocence to adulthood. As they mature, we're on call to deal with 'soul emergencies' as I call them; those challenges they face, and we respond to. For this noble role, we are in need of continual spiritual development. We're leading them, we're protecting them, we're answering their philosophical questions (and young children have plenty of them too). It's taxing, tiring but also the greatest privilege.

What Might Investing in Ourselves Look Like?

It will look different for each of us, but the goal is the same: closeness to our *Rabb*, seeking His pleasure, relying on Him, pleasing Him, asking of Him, being aware of Him. The routes to replenishing are many. I'll start on the broad common ground from my experience, as one mother to another who's lived the constant demands and responsibilities.

The Soulscape

Create a soul-nourishing environment. It's not only our children who are like sponges, soaking up what they hear and see – we're the same. The only difference is we have the ability to choose our environment and our young children don't as they depend on us. When we feel spiritually depleted, it's time to find company that help our hearts, minds and souls; company that elevates our thoughts to align ourselves with what pleases our *Rabb*. Whether it's a study-group, a local regular class, an online talk, or meeting good friends who prioritise what Allah (﷽) and His Messenger (ﷺ) love, make plans to go forward. Our *Rabb* set the criterion of what's good for us right here:

> *And keep your soul content with those who call on their Sustainer morning and evening, seeking His countenance; and let not your eyes pass beyond them, seeking the pomp and glitter of this life; nor obey any whose heart We have permitted to neglect the remembrance of Us, one who follows his own desires, whose case has gone beyond all bounds.*[40]

The great theologian and jurist Ibn Qayyim al-Jawziyyah in his book *al-Fawā'id* compared the mind to a revolving mill. What we put into it, is what we'll find:

> Certainly, Allah, the Almighty has created the mind just like a mill, which does not stop and has to have something to grind. If grain is put into it, it would grind it, and if soil is put into it or pebbles, it would also grind them. Therefore, thoughts and ideas that occur in the mind are like the grain that is put in the

40 *Sūrah al-Kahf* 18: 28.

mill, and the mill can never remain without working. Therefore, there are some people whose mill grinds grain to produce flour in order to benefit themselves and other people, but the bulk of them grind sand, pebbles, straw, etc. When it is time for kneading and baking, the reality becomes apparent to him.[41]

Hasten to Ṣalāh, Hasten to Success

The *adhān* had the answer all along. Mothers and *ṣalāh* deserves a whole article in itself! On a daily basis, it is far from our ideal as our children's needs are constant depending on their stages. Occasionally though, we should ring-fence a special, longer appointment time with our Lord on our prayer mat. If there is help around, arrange a child-free time whenever you can to be undisturbed.

We can aim, little by little, to extend our normal *ṣalāh* time to create a state of mind whereby standing in the presence of the Creator, Our Sustainer, is prioritised above all else. Dress for the occasion; standing in front of the King of kings, the Owner of this universe, is the grandest presentation we can make. Gather spiritual tools around you; your *muṣḥaf*, a *du'ā'* book, *tasbīḥ* or whatever helps you. Alternatively, be minimalist – look for a new spot in your home, a space where there's more natural light and you can feel the sun. And on entering that *ṣalāh*, think only of your soul and your *Rabb*, that the ground your forehead touches is where we all will be returning, until our final destination.

41 Ibn al-Qayyim, *Al-Fawā'id*, trans. by Umm Al Qura, Bayan Translation Services (Al Mansura: 2004) p.291

Explore the voluntary ṣalāh, the *nawāfil*, and see which one might be possible for you to do. And gradually that can become a habit; a route for your spiritual sustenance.

The Qur'ān Connection

We live in a time of endless online resources to help us recite, understand and memorise the Qur'ān. For some, this works, while for others a teacher is necessary as a point of human contact. Give yourself what you gravitate towards; memorisation, *tafsīr*, daily recitation. We are fortunate to have access now to so many compilations of *sūrah*s to recite on a regular basis, especially at blessed times such as *fajr*.

The *āyāt* of tranquillity and protection are personal favourites. How can hearing the beautiful recitation of these *āyāt* do anything but help us? One of the miracles of the Qur'ān is how the same *āyāt* are relevant to such a diverse audience, and how over time we take new lessons from them again and again.

> *And We reveal of the Qur'ān that which is a healing and a mercy to the believers.*[42]

Calling Out

Du'ā', this intimate calling out to *al-Samī' al-Baṣīr*, the All-Hearing and the All-Seeing, is literally the life-giver for our souls. It is described as 'the essence of worship'. It liberates us from the confines of our understanding, to reach out to

42 *Sūrah al-Isrā'* 17: 82.

the One for our every need: emotional, spiritual, practical. This invitation gives us a formula to elevate our *du‘ā'*, and this in itself enriches our spiritual self.

> The Messenger of Allah (ﷺ) said: 'The closest that the servant is to Allah is when he is prostrating to Him, so increase your supplications then.'[43]

Contemplation

'Tafakkur' is the practice of deeply reflecting and thinking about the signs of the Creator around us. Allah (ﷻ) tells us directly to spend time contemplating His signs in creation through vivid descriptions of natural phenomena.

The first of these 'signs' is our bodies: we are the most amazing of creation! Our very heartbeat, where every second our blood pulsates through our veins, is a miracle. Our skin is a miracle in its different layers; our eyes – the cones and rods, the nerves, the pupil, the processing of colour – all testify to the Glory of our Lord. Go through the magnificence of His signs and His names in connection to these.

Contemplate His signs in nature. It doesn't need to be an exotic location to gain soul food through His creation. Blades of grass, trees lining the pavement, weeds between cracks in a wall, daisies and corn chamomile sprouting in random green spaces – they are all *āyāt* of His magnificence and reminders to be thankful.

---

43 *Ṣaḥīḥ Muslim.*

The seasons shift and gift us displays of creation to appreciate. The passionate work of the bees and ants and flies speak volumes to our souls, if only we give them a door to enter. They give us beauty and hope. They teach us lessons. They awaken our senses and connect us back to truths held in the earth.

Seeking Forgiveness

There's no doubt that we all sin. Accumulating our mistakes – intentional or not – weigh us down. How can we reduce the baggage and travel light? The answer is *istighfār*: sincerely seeking Allah's (﷾) forgiveness. Again, we need to make some space to polish our hearts. Our beloved *Rasūl Allāh* (ﷺ) was promised Paradise yet sought forgiveness *seventy times a day*. So what about us?

The one who (regularly) seeks forgiveness, Allah (﷾) will relieve him of every burden and make from every discomfort an outlet, and He will provide for him from (sources) he never could imagine.[44]

And the other side of this coin is forgiving others. Just as we like to be forgiven, why hold on to grudges that pull us down? Letting go of the past and moving on makes space for our spiritual growth.

44 *Sunan Abū Dāwūd.*

Reliance

Some spiritual depletion comes when we feel overcome by a particular problem or situation. There are problems in life we can do something directly about, there are others we have no power over. *'Tawakkul'* – reliance on Allah (ﷻ), another strengthening concept in our *dīn* – can rescue us at these times.

In times of stress, we forget the exquisite light *tawakkul* brings into our lives. It encompasses the realisation that everything happens with His Permission and trusting that solutions will come through His Mercy, which in turn brings tranquillity to our hearts. We remember that Allah (ﷻ), the One we wholly rely on, is always available to us to turn to. *Tawakkul* is a revitalising spring for a parched soul.

Ibn al-Qayyim wrote, in his discussion on ailments and spiritual cures, that internalising our lack of ownership over Allah's (ﷻ) creation was a way of coping with a variety of losses. He observed, 'the joys of this world are a dream or a passing shadow. If the world makes you laugh a little, it makes you cry a lot. If it delights a day, it torments a lifetime.'[45] This was to emphasise how expecting long term ease in this world is futile, and accepting hardships and loss is part of keeping a balance between this life and the next in the Hereafter.

I know you'll gain so much from this issue where our insightful writers go into more details about this subject. So, I end here where I started: check in with your soul. It is

45 Perho, Irmeli. "Excessive Emotions as Illnesses of the Soul." *Studia Orientalia Electronica* 74 (1995): 130-143. p.141

what will remain after all else passes. To care for it isn't an indulgence, it's an obligation.

> Oh Allah, grant to my soul its sense of righteousness and purify it, for You are the Best purifier thereof. You are its Protecting friend and its Guardian.[46]

your Soulful Mama Editor,
Asiyah Salim.

46 *Ṣaḥīḥ Muslim.*

21

Dear Mother
who is educating
her daughter

From:

Nimra

Learning Assistant

Local Secondary School

Educating our next generation

How are you, dear Faheema?

I'm writing to you as struggling every day for our families can sure get lonely. We've got great company when the nice bits happen, like birthdays, Eid, the first day of a new class and all the other little milestones we celebrate together. The rest of the time, it's hard work, like what you're doing to educate your daughters, year in, year out. As we couldn't talk much the other day, I thought I'd write to you instead. At least in this letter I can share some thoughts as you battle on so courageously.

It's all too easy to take the education some of us had for granted. I'm guilty of that, maybe because I had the opportunities given to me, rather than having to fight for them. On the other side now, as a parent, I can see how the choices we make have such a big effect on our children. It weighs me down some days, this responsibility, wondering if I've done enough, or made the right decisions.

In the brief exchanges we have outside the school, or shops, your eyes burn with a passion to give your daughters – four energetic daughters bursting with potential – the chances in life you didn't have. You tend to be rushing around when I see you, with an urgency to see them gather up their tools and shape their lives with their own hands, as though these tools will vanish if not gripped tightly. In our exchanges you express how desperately you want them to have the opportunity to think, choose and grow. You seem ready to speed off in any direction to help them. I so admire this. Your fast pace has other reasons too.

Your eldest daughter carries this same passion. The few times I've taught her, I noticed her own brand of steely resolve in the greyish blue rim around her iris. I noticed how her mind would drift momentarily looking past me, beyond the paper and pen, out past the opaque blinds to the free movement of the clouds, far beyond the confines of the boxed lives around her. It's as if those fluffy formations promised her a better future. She once asked me out of the blue, 'Miss, if someone wants to study law, do they have to go uni' or is there any other way?'. Not long after, her gaze returned to the extract we were working on, and she plunged in earnestly, taking it apart line by line.

Recently, when you and I met by chance at the grocery shop, you mentioned the next round of secondary school entrance tests you desperately wanted your youngest daughter to prepare for. As always, you were pressed for time and spoke with the urgency of someone reporting from a crime scene: flustered and edgy. I was impressed with the speed at which you could relay so much information – as quickly as possible – or else you'll need to explain your absence to him.

I know you needed to offload what was troubling you, as though you'd burst otherwise – so out it flowed. Thankfully it was quiet there that morning in the detergent aisle, when you repeated his words to me. I remember them well.

'All the schools are the same,' he says, 'you just wasting your time with stupid tests. Just a waste – you just see, she'll fail anyway. Look at me, I earn money don't I? I didn't do all that rubbish, looking for good schools. Those schools just there to make money, 'cos government gotta give them money and then us parents gotta take hard earned cash and throw it down the drain on uniform, bags, those trips and all that rubbish ... Tell 'er to get a job when she's 16. Earn money like me. Then she's gonna get shaadi, have kids and be useless like you anyway ... What after school class rubbish. Hah, you just see you're wasting money.'

You've obviously heard it so often it spilled out like projectile vomiting. You looked at me for a response to his monologue. It's as though you needed to hear that he wasn't right, was he? That this was wrong, wasn't it, to think like this? Hearing the same crushing thing time and time again, it's easy to start believing it, no matter how absurd and insulting it is.

I was in shock, and I didn't know what to say in that moment. All I could do was encourage you to keep going, keep replacing what he says with what you're doing. To keep up your determination and action.

There was just enough time, in the two minutes before you sped off, to tell me how you trust in Allah (ﷻ). He is the One Who decides all matters, so you surrender to His Will, no matter what their father says. 'I've got to do their *tarbiyah*,' you concluded. This is your fragrance to replace the stench.

You keep the embers burning, growing quietly inside and power on. Of course there is always the threat of the light going out with the scoffs and jibes of her father: He advises with such parental authority, it baffles me that the same person is totally absent from his children's daily lives and particularly their schooling. These small human beings he has fathered are supposed to be thankful for his presence. How are these opinions supposed to help and guide them?

Remember, Faheema, that education is a right – a God given right for your daughter. There is no question about this, as it is Our Creator, *al-Khāliq*, The King of Kings, *al-Malik*, Who revealed to our noble Prophet (ﷺ), the instruction to

> *Read! Read in the name of your Sustainer Who created. He created the human beings from clustered germ-cells. Read and your Sustainer is Most Generous, Who taught by the pen. Taught the human being what he knew not.*[47]

Keep your heart warmed with the reminder that our noble mothers (ﷺ), included women who studied. Our Mother 'Ā'ishah (ﷺ) is the best of examples. Her knowledge in the field of medicine and poetry were well known from when she was young. As she grew older, her knowledge grew in the areas of *fiqh*, history and genealogy, each of which is a highly respected field. She (ﷺ) taught several of the Companions of the Prophet (ﷺ) and narrated over two thousand *ḥadīth*. 'Ā'ishah (ﷺ) praised the women of the Anṣār for their spirit of enquiry and learning, saying: 'How praiseworthy are the women of the Anṣār that their modesty does not prevent them from attempts at learning and the acquisition of

47 *Sūrah al-'Alaq* 96: 1-5.

knowledge.'[48]

If I take *ḥadīth* scholarship as one example, Faheema, what does it tell us about gaining knowledge when we remember that the noble wives of *Rasūl Allāh* (ﷺ), Ḥafṣah (﵂) and Maymūnah (﵂), narrated several *ḥadīth*s and Umm Salamah (﵂), related over 300 *ḥadīth*s? While Makkah and Madinah continued to be thriving places of education for men and women, the legacy of women's scholarship in Qur'ānic studies and *ḥadīth* continued for centuries. Thousands of Muslim women studied and taught in homes, mosques and schools across Egypt, Syria, Iraq, Iran, Turkmenistan, Uzbekistan and Afghanistan. Famous women scholars also taught in Jerusalem, Delhi, Cordoba and across the North African region. Over time, thousands of women continued with scholarship in *ḥadīth* alone.[49]

I'm not saying this is the only area Muslim women have studied. It's one example, though, that reinforces our history of women being educated. Education is an endless voyage which includes so much more than the subjects in the school curriculum. As you mentioned, it is their *tarbiyah* you're concerned about. And *tarbiyah* is vast; it's nurturing their character, their way of thinking and looking at the world, nurturing their heart and soul, building their relationship with Allah (ﷻ) and His creation; people and the planet! That is what educating them means. And your efforts in all these directions are known to Allah (ﷻ), The All-Seeing. So yes, it is tough to do this, and it is tougher when you're making the effort without the support you and

48 *Ṣaḥīḥ Muslim.*
49 Mohammad Akram Nadwi, *Al-Muḥaddithāt:* The Women Scholars in Islam, Interface Publications Ltd, (2013, Oxford UK)

your daughters deserve.

Keep strong, Faheema. I see how you work hard to fit in your tailoring work to support extra lessons and resources for your girls. One day you'll see all this effort turn them into four educated young women. And *in shā' Allāh*, with your sincerity, I hope you'll find *barakah* placed in all that you're doing for them – a goodness and growth from Allah (ﷻ) that is far beyond something we can define in a word or two. When our efforts are transformed with '*barakah*', incredible things happen.

While the seeds of encouragement you are giving them now will not bear fruit today, or tomorrow, or even next year, the time will come to reap the rewards, *in shā' Allāh*. Hang in there! One day you'll find the harvest of your efforts and the struggle to educate them will be over. Your daughters will know the way to support their own learning with the blessing of Allah (ﷻ). It's a shame when the person who should support you and his daughters, is busier putting up barriers. I'm sorry if I've over-stepped a line saying this.

Keep educating and nurturing your daughters' minds, keep fighting for their education. They will succeed, *in shā' Allāh*. Keep going. My *du'ā's* are with you.

From a daughter who received an education,
Now a mother educating her daughter,
Your ally,
Nimra.

22

DEAR MOTHER
HANGING IN THERE AT
EID ṢALĀH

From:
An older Mother
A few spaces down,
At Eid *ṣalāh jamā'at*

Beloved sister, my *salām*s to you and Eid *Mubārak*,

Both you and your family look the picture – a picture of health, togetherness and happiness, *māshā' Allāh*! It's charming and hopeful.

But there's something behind your strained smile some of us mothers recognise. We know that if a feather's weight more stress comes your way, your inner dam will burst, the tears will flow and even you won't know where they've sprung from. Right now, you can hold things together until the end of the *khuṭbah* (sermon) and the greetings are exchanged.

I guess hundreds of fellow mothers understand, standing in Eid *ṣalāh*, in sheer exhaustion. Some might think you're looking pensive because it's the end of the blessed month, slipping away for another year. For sure, that's part of the emotion too. But we both know there's something else going on: the burn-out from our expectations of how Eid 'should be'.

It doesn't start this way though. Each year we evaluate how to improve the quality of our *'ibādah*, how to reorganise life around the fasts and family commitments, how to fit in charitable causes and work on our personal blind-spots.

163

Each year as the month approaches and the realities of life just happen – most of which is out of our control (who plans for a flat tyre, a boiler replacement or a squirrel nest in the roof *in* Ramadan?) – the intention to improve is challenged at every turn. And if something major, like medical issues crop up, then it can feel like a downward spiral, from all those noble pre-Ramadan plans into managing the mundane.

Thinking back, I remember gradually getting into gear by the end of the first week. I'd feel accomplished for managing the younger kids well and some teenage situations I'd normally lose my cool with. Getting it together, personal *'ibādah*, spinning the domestic plates; it starts to feel as though I was reaping some benefits of the month. Each year I'd tell myself, as if it was for the first time: that the elder ones remain themselves. A switch isn't flipped in Ramadan to change them into considerate, caring individuals. The only difference is we're expected to have infinite amounts of patience and benevolence towards their attitudes.

There were good days when an impromptu conversation turned into a rich discussion where they'd all be involved, and our spiritual selves aligned with the Month of Mercy. These precious times kept me going when there were not so good days.

It could be similar for you too, looking at the ages of your daughters sat next to you. On the not so good days, the time set aside for reading the Qur'ān would evaporate when a neighbour would pop by with a long complaint about the state of the rubbish collection on your road. What do you do? You can't ignore them, especially as this neighbour rarely stops by like this. You stand there, reminding yourself that He knows your intentions. Another *juz'* behind. This is your Ramadan. Your husband's Qur'ān reading is on target, carved into the quiet before and after work. That is his Ramadan.

As a Mother, you know you're not only doing your Ramadan. It's your children's Ramadan you feel you are carrying too, especially the older ones who are actually fasting. The younger ones you encourage along in their *ṣalāh*, in short stints of 'fasting', and they're quite willing to participate. The pressure about the 'Ramadan look' with the homemade this and the hand printed that doesn't help either.

The pressure mounts and mounts and the sleep deprived, emotionally drained state of our 'mother mind' is fragile. From my own and my friends' past experience, when everyone's gone to bed the night before Eid, you still have a list of at least nine more things to get done before heading off to the *ṣalāh* in the morning. To keep the rising tide of frustration mixed with tiredness at bay I'd remind myself about those in worse situations than my own. Lonely people, grieving people, homeless people, displaced people, refugee people – they have Eid tomorrow too, and they must make do. This logic, whilst true, is also lost a bit because I'd be too tired to think it through properly and these thoughts would be left dangling.

Eid *Ṣalāh* is approached with this feeling of being overstretched. It's not just within your household where there are things to do. There's all the communicating with both sides of relatives to make plans that keep everyone happy; the gift buying, the Eid day outfit organising even if you're not buying new ones.

After years of being exhausted on Eid morning, I finally conceded it was down to expecting too much of myself and the Eid day trimmings – and, of course, sleep deprivation. I had to have a Q&A with myself: what is *iḥsān* in *'ibādah* (excellence in worship) and how does that feel? What is perfectionism in the home? (I know, it seems kind of obvious enough that these two things are different when I write it out like that). What's the difference? What are realistic expectations for our children's happiness on Eid? What am I teaching them about values and what matters on Eid day?

It took time to work through all that and realise that the priority is striving for *iḥsān* – that earnest and sincere *'ibādah*. Minimising distractions and not doing it for anything else but seeking the closeness to and reward from Our Sustainer, Most High. I had to separate that from stress inducing 'perfectionist' tendencies. They are totally different, I had to tell myself this over and over.

I settled for making an effort on the Eid front but compartmentalising the time and resources that would go into it. And most importantly, being content with doing what I could within those limits. Making myself accept that the food, home, clothes, gifts for neighbours was good enough in the allotted time.

At the same time, I had to think ahead and answer the values question: what is really going to matter to the children? Was I giving them too many expectations and then setting up a problem for times when there might not be as many games, or outings or presents? The spirit of Eid is joy, sharing and gratitude. It's a sacred day of meeting family, friends, and community people. The spirit of Ramadan is gaining closeness to Allah (ﷻ) through focusing on the Qur'ān's message. It really isn't that complicated, I told myself. So how had things got this frantic for me that I'd end up shattered and in a daze by Eid morning?

Figuring out my answers felt liberating from my self-made problems. I made some practical changes too: delegated more inside the house, took short cuts for some shopping things, learnt to say fewer 'yeses' during Ramadan. It all helped. Sister, we're all of us going to have different conversations with ourselves. But I'm sharing mine with you, as I'm now a few years down the line from those days. I hope it helps you somehow.

It's there, in the stillness of the Eid *jamā'ah*, listening to the *khuṭbah*, that you find relief for the bundle of emotions weighing you down. In the words of the *khaṭīb*, it all aligns. Relief replaces regrets, a clear message calms your thoughts.

It's here, stood in rows, in the stillness of the Eid *Ṣalāh*, facing Our Sustainer, that we face the real purpose of it all. One of the many benefits of *ṣalāh* is our physical presence, facing the *qiblah*, every limb surrendering to our *Rabb*, our Sustainer, *al-Laṭīf*, the Subtle One, who sees and knows the minutest details of our lives. It's here, forehead on the ground and heart open to Him (ﷻ), that we start again.

The Eid *Ṣalāh*, whilst being the landing patch for our tiredness, is also the source of energy for our soul. Beyond this beautiful communal *sujūd* and communal *qiyām*, we can return home with the comforting knowledge that no matter how our hours and days are going, each *ṣalāh* time is an invitation to realign, re-purpose, re-measure and restart. And then, with that renewal, we can once again step out into the world.

With love,
Another mother

23

DEAR MOTHER
'STUCK IN THE CONFLICT'

From:
Sofia
Your virtual friend
Parenting alongside you,
Another state geographically
The same state maternally
The World Wide Web

How's it going Lynna?

I hope you are doing well. It was good to have the two weeks offline, even though I thought it would be impossible! I missed our conversations, so it's great to sit down and write to you properly now. It's done me good though – feels like I've been away on a holiday. This 'technology fast' has been great for growing headspace.

It gave me space to think through all sorts of things, including what you wrote regarding feeling like you're 'stuck in conflict' on a permanent basis. There's no joy in life when it feels like the constant struggle you described. I used to think that's just how it is as a parent at a certain stage of our kids' development. But now I know it doesn't have to be like this.

Even though my two have come out of that phase (by some miracle, no less!), I have enough memories to recall the way the clashes just consumed my brain. It was like ink on blotting paper, thirsty to cover the whole surface, from my thinking to feeling and rational self. So, yes, I got it when you said it feels like there's no way out. And no, it's not wrong some days to feel like you just can't stand it anymore. That you want to hand in your 'letter of resignation' as you put it, to move on and start life all over again, anonymously. I think if more mothers were honest, they'd admit to feeling this at some point.

It's that treadmill: a conflict, attempts to resolve it, then before you know it, another conflict. And so it goes on and on. You wake up thinking *today will be different*. And it is for a bit. Until 11.30 am and then a simple instruction (at least in my head it was simple), turns into a historical analysis of your teen 'never being trusted', 'never being good enough', or the classic 'treated like a baby', and the treadmill is in full motion again.

Thank goodness that nowadays there are plenty of parenting coaches and online groups, besides the books, with strategies on how to improve the situations we face. I hope the workshop you signed up to is helpful. Some of the IG lives and webinars I've watched (before the online break!) had sound practical advice. Shame it's after I've gone through this phase. Remind me to send you a couple of links.

One of the good things that came out of my online break was a book I read which I've been wanting to tell you about. I came across it at the library, thinking that it was about general relationships (you know about the issues I'm having) only to find it's brilliant on parent-child relationships as well. Even with my cynical eyes, not willing to accept the 'hype' about trends, this book is definitely going to help me with all family communications, from the elders to the youngsters and those in between.

It's called *The Power of Discord: why the ups and downs of relationships are the secret to building intimacy, resilience and trust* by Dr Ed Tronick & Dr Claudia M. Gold. Both writers are experienced clinicians and researchers. Their years of experience with their clients come through in every chapter. You know I don't have clinical knowledge at all, Lynna, and they *do* describe experiments and research. But I still got so much out of it because all the points they make come through stories of everyday people's challenges, mostly of their clients and other narratives they've collected.

The main, hopeful message I took away was that healthy relationships are not found when there is perfect alignment between parent and child or husband and wife, but rather when there is a series of 'mismatches' and 'repairs' which create trust and long-lasting resilience and growth. There are so many points to talk about, but for now, I've narrowed them down to a few to share with you.

The book starts with explaining the 'still face experiment' (attributed to Tronick) where a mother adopts a 'still face', in that she shows no reaction to her baby for a few moments. The effect of this on the baby is fascinating as he/she makes several attempts to get the mother's attention and make a connection (referred to as 'repair') until they give up. The baby's repeated reactions to the mother's lack of engagement opens up a discussion that goes throughout the book on how babies' brains develop and the way they can 'read' facial expressions. I wish this was a part of compulsory education before we had kids.

The authors extract the meaning that it's innate from birth onwards to want to make a connection with the main care giver, and even a very young baby will make attempts to 'reconnect' as a matter of instinct. With that as a premise, the book throws light on so many aspects of our daily relationships we can repair if we are aware of what's going on during a 'mismatch'. I'm going to switch here to making a list, as there's so much I want to share! Some variety for once – hang in there, I promise you'll relate to some of it! Here are my main 'takeaways':

1. Mismatch is the norm: I was relieved when I read this as I guess you'll be too! It's not like you must be best friends or compatible personalities with your child to have a healthy relationship (people projecting this on social media helps this myth circulate). That myth being bust, was gold.

The authors used practical research, anecdotes and practitioner theories to show how not being aligned for 70% of the interactions they observed between mothers and their children is normal, with only 30% of interactions being in sync. As long as those instances of 'mismatch' are repaired quickly, then trust and understanding builds. Even if they are repaired months or years later through addressing the 'disconnect', there's still every opportunity to heal and move on. The sooner it's repaired the better.

2. Aiming for 'Good Enough': I found their discussion on the 'Necessary Imperfection', at a time of perfect everything, especially online, hugely reassuring. As the authors put it:

'This drive for perfection seems to be fuelling the struggles of a generation of adults who are diagnosed with mental illness. Developers of the perfectionism scale have found over decades of research that perfectionism correlates with depression, anxiety, eating disorders and other emotional problems.'[50]

They cite the culture of trying to 'fix' everything as part of the problem. Instead, they go to lengths to argue 'imperfection' is the messy norm of relationships, and there's nothing wrong with that. Rather, it's much healthier.

The section on the 'Too Good Mother' shows that expecting to have the 'right answer' to fix our children's problem or attitude leads to anxious and nervous parenting and trying to control the children's behaviour. In contrast, the authors say the 'good enough' mother who fails to meet her child's need immediately does a better job by making space for the 'messiness' of their developmental stage. Working through the 'mismatch' and 'repair', they contend, develops a healthier long-term relationship of growth and trust without the stress of perfection.

Remember all our conversations about the guilt of not knowing what to do? Well, now I realise our not knowing immediately was a good and natural thing. We weren't failing!

3. Overcoming childhood baggage: Do you remem-ber that podcast we discussed a while back about childhood trauma and how it affects people differently? We got into a deep debate about

50 Dr Ed Tronick & Dr Claudia M Gold, *The Power of Discord* (New York: Little Brown Spark, 2020)

whether the term is getting overused and where the middle ground lies. Well, their chapter on 'When Meanings Go Awry' answers so many of our questions. This extract puts it well:

'Countless moment to moment interactions over the course of development are like raindrops that shape the landscape of your sense of yourself, both alone and in relation to others. An experience becomes traumatic when a person remains committed to a fixed meaning and stays stuck in a pattern of disconnection and miscommunication.'[51]

The message in this chapter is that with the right help – like psychotherapy – older children and adults can rewire the meanings they have attached to certain experiences and bring new meanings to new relationships. That spelled hope to me. In discussing the everyday 'chronic unrepaired mismatch', such as repeatedly experiencing isolation or humiliation as a child, the authors demonstrated through narratives how people have overcome fixed meanings from their past and transformed family relationships they were struggling with.[52] Relatable examples include disagreements between parents about children's sleep routines and solving clashes when communicating with teens.

Finally, even though there are more things I could say, reading the ninth chapter on 'Healing in a Mosaic of Moments' was like having a talk with a positive, practical friend we all need. The authors showed practical ways of

51 p. 147.
52 p. 146.

using creative outlets and communication with new people in our lives, as they explain here:

> By immersing ourselves in a new set of interactions over time, with hundreds of thousands of moments of engaging with the mess, we create new meanings by moving through mismatch to repair. And as we have seen, the meanings we make of ourselves are not only in words and thoughts.[53]

Learning about how 'repair' works and why it sometimes doesn't happen was the most fascinating lesson in this book for me. It made me look at times and situations where I repeatedly didn't 'repair' and allowed disconnection to take root in unhealthy ways.

The authors dive deep into the myriad reasons disconnection doesn't get repaired, and there are common mind-sets we can easily identify with. Not all examples are about parent-child relationships, but many are. In those examples you really get a wake-up call about how 'seeing' the traits of another family member in your child is one reason you might distance yourself from repairing, for example.

So, while you, I and hundreds of mothers may be riddled with guilt and feeling inadequate, this book helps to see clashes as the 'messiness' of building honest resilience and stronger relationships. It gives hope, as long as there's a willingness to do the work it takes each time to repair.

I'll stop here – I didn't realise I'd have so much to say. In all it gave me some realistic ideas to deal with my difficulties

53 p. 214.

that I told you about. A bonus was that there was so much about parent-child relationships too. I'll post you the book if you'd like to read it!

Loads of love,
Sofia
xxx

24

DEAR MOTHER
OF TWO GENERATIONS

Dearest Urooj,

You may be surprised that I'm writing to you. It's good to be in touch with our short mobile phone messages, but they disappear too fast for my liking. So, I decided to pick up the pen, take my time and write to my heart's content.

Thank you for the warm hospitality you both extended to me, making my month in your home a truly valuable time. I missed your father sorely before I came, it's been too long a gap since we've visited each other. Once I was there though, it was back to our normal selves. It's intriguing how I might think of something unknown to him, yet he brings the very same topic up. Even with his health taking a turn, he remembered my favourite lines from a poem we learnt in our youth. Here's how it starts:

Ata Hai Yaad Mujh Ko Guzra Huwa Zamana
Woh Bagh Ki Baharain, Woh Sub Ka Chehchana.

I am constantly reminded of the bygone times
Those garden's springs, those chorus of chimes.

Azadiyan Kahan Woh Ab Apne Ghonsle Ki
Apni Khushi Se Ana, Apni Khushi Se Jana.

Gone are the freedoms of our own nests
Where we could come and go at our own pleasure.

Lagti Hai Chot Dil Per, Ata Hai Yad Jis Dam
Shabnaam Ke Ansuon Per Kaliyon Ka Muskarana.

My heart aches the moment I think
Of the buds' smile at the dew's tears.

It's from the *Parinde ki Fariyad* (The Bird's Complaint), has
he recited it to you? If not, remind him to do so, he still
recalls the whole thing.[54] We thoroughly enjoyed sharing
the memories of our childhood growing up in Qaisar Bagh,
our school days and reliving the stories about our beloved
relatives and parents who are no longer with us. I will cherish
this month with you forever!

While I stayed over, I also witnessed that the demands on
you have increased from all directions. Since my brother's
health has declined, I noticed his increasing frustration and
the effect on you. His happiness comes from your lovely
family, this is his entire world of contentment. Ageing and
illness change a person's communication.

As your children are older, they need you in new, more
complex ways. At the same time your father's needs are

54 Muhammad Iqbal, *The Bird's Complaint* (for Children), in: *Bang-e-
Dara – The Call of the Marching Bell*, The Iqbal Academy Pakistan
www.allamaiqbal.com http://www.allamaiqbal.com/poetry.php?-
bookbup=22&orderno=12&lang_code=en&lang=2&conType=en

increasing. How perplexing this world is sometimes; time inches us elders on, usually painfully, while the young surrender willingly to the hourglass flowing, willing it go faster and faster if they could.

As I sat beside your father, in the temperate, sunny conservatory (I enjoyed your choice of vibrant patterned fabric for the newly upholstered armchair), I saw your struggle in broad daylight. They may look glazed, as I squint behind my thick lenses, but my eyes noted how your responsibilities have grown in the past two years. How do you manage them?

There is clearly much more on your mind now. As the children grow, their carefree playfulness is replaced with a mixture of opportunities and worry. When I raised my children alone, with two of them teenagers, those were the hardest years of my life. Some of that time I was lecturing at the University of Lucknow, other years I dropped that and worked limited hours as a general doctor. Once your cousins were settled in their high school, I did both jobs; at home and outside. It wasn't easy keeping the two worlds in tandem. Home itself is a universe of needs.

I understand that at any given moment of the day, you carry a bundle of worries alongside the increased physical work. Their clubs and masjid classes. Co-ordinating your part-time studies with their eye appointments, their dental check-ups, their school trip meetings, pick-up and drop-offs to friends' houses. My memory can't even hold on to all the things I saw you do in one day! May the Almighty bless you with the strength and health to carry out your responsibilities to them and yourself.

With all the pulls and pushes on you by the people you love dearly, it can become overwhelming. As my treasured niece, I share my thoughts out of concern for you, thinking about how you make time each day for rest. You're blessed to have a good husband and wonderful father for your children, doing what he can alongside you. He is blessed to have your endless abilities to keep the family running! Even with you working together as a team, your health should get some special attention. Life keeps changing and, in response, our need for balance in our lives evolves too. The essence of balance in this *ḥadīth* is one I love dearly:

> You have a duty to your Lord, you have a duty to your body, you have a duty to your family, so you should give each one its rights.[55]

When your father and I listened to the radio while I was there, we heard talk about 'self-care', 'retail-therapy' and that other one: 'mindfulness'. It's a strange world, I thought as we listened. First, they create the imbalances by neglecting essential areas of health for half a century, and then they spend the second half trying to rectify them. I see they're trying to put it right now. The newspaper columns too dedicate space to these ideas. I may look too old to be up to date with these fashionable theories, but many principles from my years lecturing in the Department of *Ṭibb-e Yūnānī* have stayed with me. Why do I mention this? I want to share a little more about it, perhaps you'll find it useful both for your own and your father's health.

Yūnānī is the Arabic word for Greek and *ṭibb* means medicine, so this medical system originated from Greek

55 *Ṣaḥīḥ al-Bukhārī*: 1968.

works which Ibn Sīnā and many other Persian and Arab scholars developed further. The *Kitāb al-Shifā* (Book of Healing) and *al-Qānūn fi'l-Ṭibb* (The Canon of Medicine), both by Ibn Sīnā, are well known. This traditional practice developed alongside scientific knowledge and conventional medicine and is still practised across South Asia, South East Asia and the Middle East. The next time you travel with your family to any of these regions, you could find out more. The principles of these works run through communities as a given norm of daily living, especially in the smaller towns.

Yūnānī therapy is holistic, it gives importance to psychological and environmental factors which affect our physical health. Your day with young children has different pressures on you; sometimes the children make you happy, other times stressed, or even angry. Normally this is manageable. But with caring for a parent as well, as you do for your father, there is a longer-term emotional strain. This link between our emotional, spiritual and physical states is explored in detail by the classical medical scholars who wrote on holistic treatments.

The years I combined *Yūnānī* principles – connecting diet, emotional health, sleep patterns, the type of company a person keeps and their exposure to the elements – in my practice, were the most fulfilling years of my medical service. That was when I felt I could treat the 'whole' person. While we treated medical symptoms with conventional drugs and treatments, for many other conditions we used herbs and mineral compounds.

Now I hear the term 'social prescribing', and that was something else we used: those everyday changes to someone's life to bring balance by improving their environment. We took it for granted that there's a huge benefit gained to our state of being when a person has regular good company or spends time in nature. Another radio programme we listened to called this 'ecotherapy'. In these modern times, I see there's creative, new ways in which people are finding a balance in their lives.

As for the complexity of your phase – being mother to two generations – I only know half of it. When I raised my children alone, I attempted being both parents. My elderly parents were in another part of the country cared for by your two youngest uncles, so I didn't share that responsibility. But, as a single mother, often, I felt I could barely fulfil my role. It was a long and lonely journey of survival in the beginning. In those days I realised just how isolated a single parent feels. If it wasn't for the kind neighbours helping me while I worked, I don't know what would have happened to us. I always make *du'ā'* those neighbours are rewarded for their kindness and compassion. Maybe they helped me more because I was widowed young, without any close family around me, watching me struggle and seeing I couldn't manage. It was unusual in those days to stay where I was, and not move closer to relatives. The reality was the quality of education for your cousins and the opportunity for me to work was much better if we stayed where we were. Eventually I found reliable home help on a regular basis and our situation improved.

You're an expert juggler, Urooj, managing the needs of two generations, making the impossible look straightforward! But remember, there is no shame in seeking help – it can come in so many ways. Consider it as a way of looking after yourself too. A friend's son in England has found local services that have supported them greatly with caring for their elderly mother's needs. Even though they do their best as a family for her, there are specific health related groups that give practical help and solutions.

Whichever way you find to care for yourself in the midst of the small storms that come and go in life, remember that while your work and role is highly valued, your wellbeing is equally important. The Divine words from Our Creator and Sustainer, come to my mind whenever I think about the stages we grow through:

> *Nay! I call to witness the sunset's fleeting afterglow,*
> *And the night and what it unfolds,*
> *And by the moon, as it grows to fullness,*
> *That you are bound to move onwards from stage to stage.*[56]

So Urooj, we are guaranteed to struggle from one phase to the next; birth to childhood, rising in our youth, climbing to adulthood, and then from that zenith of strength we gradually decline. And through these stages you do the honourable work of steadying the steps of your family, of easing their struggles, of caring for them. Allah (ﷻ) has blessed you with spiritual strength and wisdom that you pour into family relationships. There is nothing more admirable – so long as there is support for you too.

Since your father reminded me of how we exchanged lines of Iqbal's *shayri*[57] in our youth, I took out a book of his

---

56 *Sūrah al-Inshiqāq* 84: 16–19.
57 Poetry in Urdu.

selected poems, sat for years in my dishevelled, tired cabinet. I'm sharing a rediscovered favourite here: '*Aql-o-Dil* – Reason and Heart.[58] I hope it takes you on a charming journey (in your elegant armchair) the way it took me, when I sat with it again. Reading with older eyes, it means something different from the last time I read it. When you next send me a message, share your thoughts on this too.

'*Aql-o-Dil* (Reason and Heart)

Aqal Ne Aik Din Ye Dil Se Kaha
Bhoole Bhatke Ki Rahnuma Hun Main
One day reason said to the heart:
"I am a guide for those who are lost.

Hun Zameen Par, Guzr Falak Pe Mera
Dekh To Kis Qadar Rasa Hun Main
I live on earth, but I roam the skies—
just see the vastness of my reach.

Kaam Dunya Mein Rahbari Hai Mera
Misl-e-Khizr-e-Khajasta Pa Hun Main
My task in the world is to guide and lead,
I am like Khizr of blessed steps.

Hun Mufassir-e-Kitab-e-Hasti Ki
Mazhar-e-Shan-e-Kibriya Hun Main
I interpret the book of life,
And through me Divine Glory shines forth.

58 Allama Iqbal, Reason and Heart from *Bang-e-Dra* in The Poetry of Allama Iqbal, trans by Dr Muntasir Mir, ©The Iqbal Academy Government of Pakistan http://www.allamaiqbal. com/poetry.php?-bookbup=22&orderno=15&lang_ code=en&lang=2&conType=en.

Boond Ek Khoon Ki Hai Tu Lekin
Ghairat-e-Laal-e-Be Baha Hun Main.
You are no more than a drop of blood,
While I am the envy of the priceless pearl!"

Dil Ne Sun Kar Kaha Ye Sub Sach Hai
Par Mujhe Bhi To Dekh, Kya Hun Main.
The heart listened, and then said: "This is all true,
But now look at me, and see what I am.

Raaz-e-Hasti Ko Ti Samajhti Hai
Aur Ankhon Se Dekhta Hun Main!
You penetrate the secret of existence,
But I see it with my eyes.

Hai Tujhe Wasta Mazahir Se
Aur Batin Se Ashna Hun Main.
You deal with the outward aspect of things,
I know what lies within.

Ilm Tujh Se To Maarifat Mujh Se
Tu Khuda Joo, Khuda Numa Hun Main.
Knowledge comes from you, gnosis from me;
You seek God, I reveal Him.

Ilm Ki Intiha Hai Betaabi
Iss Marz Ki Magar Dawa Hun Main.
Attaining the ultimate in knowledge
only makes one restless—
I am the cure for that malady.

Shama Tu Mehfil-e-Sadaqat Ki
Husn Ki Bazm Ka Diya Hun Main.
You are the candle of the Assembly of Truth;
I am the lamp of the Assembly of Beauty.

Tu Zaman-o-Makan Se Rishta Bapa
Taeer-e-Sidra Se Ashna Hun Main.
You are hobbled by space and time,
While I am the bird in the Lotus Tree.

Kis Bulandi Pe Hai Maqam Mera
Arsh Rab-e-Jaleel Ka Hun Main!
My status is so high—
I am the throne of the God of Majesty!"

The struggle between the head and heart keeps us all intrigued. It is wonderful to rediscover these lines and share them with you.

I end now, with my *du'ā'* for your beautiful family: I pray the Almighty eases your path and theirs and grants you *barakah* in all areas of your life. *Āmīn.*

With love and admiration,
Your Aunty Sadaf

25

DEAR CHILD
WHO IS THE MOTHER

From:
Indah
An old school friend & neighbour,
The Crescent – our childhood world,
In the suburbs

My dear childhood friend,

You were just a child, Reem, when you had to be the mother.

I saw fragments of your life. As a neighbour, that's what it's like; we rarely see the whole picture. Even though I was only two years older than you, I was old enough to gather the sentences that fell carelessly between the adults. And, of course, I observed you too. It was enough to build up the life you led; sometimes carefree as a child when your mother was well, other times carrying out her role when she was ill.

Looking back, I realise I witnessed your childhood morph into motherhood; doing what you could to protect your three younger siblings. And now, years later, as I find your profile online, it all comes back, scene upon scene.

No mother, in normal circumstances, plans to give up her responsibilities. Every mother wants to be able to nurture and protect her child. Sadly, in our community at that time, mental wellness was viewed like a choice: it was a 'you can be happy if you want to', type of attitude. And generally mothers were the first to be blamed for any fractures that appeared in the family. 'They didn't take care', or 'they didn't manage the children properly' was how it was described. Few thought of asking the husband about his wife's wellbeing without judgement. All they had to do was ask, but that's not obvious always, is it?

Life is strange. Your mother, a beautiful, gregarious and generous character, from what I can remember, went through months of wellness and being visible. Those were your good times – your normal times. The times you could leave your brothers' side and not be their shadow. Then there were times (and these got increasingly long) where we never saw her and just saw your way of surviving: in the local shop as you bought bread and milk, or at the school gates where you didn't have the freedom of spirit to make up games all the way home.

And so, I felt compelled to write to you, because the memories of seeing you at school and in our neighbourhood are still so vivid. As we were two year groups in one class, it meant I saw more of your life than other neighbourhood children did. The years since then have faded some of those recollections, but the rest, I still see:

Your warm smile and compassion set you apart from the other children at school. If someone's left out, you include them in the game. If they've lost something, you help them find it. Even when Kerrie Jones was left out because she was pushing us, you'd run over to her and let her join in again.

The PE teacher pops her head around our classroom door and waves a PE bag in the air for attention. Our teacher

walks over and nods as she sees the name. Your kit is mixed up with your brothers. You run over to where it's hanging and exchange bags. As she's about to head off you call out, and hastily hand over your brother's reading book in your bag too.

The school secretary, Mrs Osman, strides in and signals to you to go to the office with her in the middle of our project time. Our teacher looks at you with a sad smile, like she's worried. You come back after five minutes and carry on making the poster with the rest of our group.

You have a friendly, caring expression and there's something tender about your eyes. Is there something they're holding back though? We know your mother's not well. Sometimes you're the quietest one in the playground. Other days you bounce around like the rest of us children.

You're usually ahead of us, walking your two little brothers home. You wait at the edge of the kerb till any grown up is about to cross and you follow them across, your brothers' hands tightly held in yours.

There is a reason your childhood is shaped like this. Though difficult and testing, there is something it is giving you, something it is laying in your hands. Only you will know what that is.

When I look at your profile picture now, I see neither the little girl's eyes nor her forehead have changed. You still have that child inside you; we all do. But the child inside you needs the nurturing, the days of freedom, the nights of security that got cut short.

Your childhood touched our lives and we carry the undercurrents of empathy in our interactions. I remember enough of the lines spoken by your eyes to know never to ignore those expressions in another child when I go about life now. And I know I need to take some action when necessary – reaching out, talking to the right people, asking questions. I mustn't turn a 'blind eye', but notice and speak up. However small the action, we all need to offer some help to that child, the child who is the mother before her time. The memory of your life and your family's struggle has kept my mind open and alive to the harsh realities so many children face around the world in different ways.

I end, trusting that He who gave us life, Our Sustainer and Creator, The One we will return to soon, will not leave you alone for a second. May the love and protection of *al-Wadūd* and *al-Ḥāfiẓ* give you the strength to rise through this. I pray your world is a better one now as an adult. I pray you are healed. I pray you are nourished in heart and soul, and there is balm to ease those scars of your childhood. I pray the strong child inside you is honoured and knows she is worthy of care and affection, of being indulged, of daydreaming.

With much love,
Your childhood neighbour,
Indah

26

DEAR MOTHER
WITH THE RADIO ON

From:
Another parent
With the radio on
Global Airwaves

*Salām*s Saba,

I'm so glad we had that tube ride together after the session last week. It's really the only time we ever find to catch up. As I promised, here's the piece I wrote a few months ago. As you'll see, it's similar to the experiences you described about hearing random news or analysis pieces when taking your teens to school, and the toll it takes on us all. I'm still thinking over whether to submit it for the 'monologue' pitch for the new online magazine that was mentioned in the seminar. Tell me what you think, please? There's still a couple of weeks till the deadline.

A Ramadan Monologue

It's 8 pm and I need to drop my second daughter off to a friend's house for a small *Ifṭār* invitation. She's been eagerly looking forward to this one; four school friends who've just finished their A-level exams and their seven years of school life together. Standing at the threshold of their future, their youth exudes eager hope, agitation, nervousness and energy all at once.

Between finishing school and discovering what their next move will be, there's an appreciation for all that is

Ramadan. It is a cushion to lean on for a while, a compass to re-orientate, a spiritual life jacket to buoy you up for the year. We set off for the 15 minute drive to her friend's house with her piling into the back seat so she can balance a dish of chicken kebabs, an overnight bag and a haul of snacks for *suḥūr* (pre-dawn meal). And that particular smile, the one reserved for friends.

The air is warm and turns spicier down the end of our road. The atmosphere is still, suspended and quieter than usual; only a car or two crawl up this steep end, as though they're doing the UK summer fast too. The radio is on before I realise; Radio Score is the default setting.

I recognise the voice. It is an imam and media analyst, K. A. He is mid-sentence and I catch the tone as it's a contentious topic. The interview morphs into a verbal match, but ever so politely. We're British, after all. Terse measured words, quick off the mark, the presenter breathes in, and the imam seizes the opportunity with another point, highlights another contradiction, snaps up the inhalation opportunity to defend. Again. Wimbledon ended last week. This interview continues the pace; back and forth, sharp and calculated. The linesmen are not impartial though.

There are other rules to this game: the questions are loaded, more like verdicts. The answers involve retorting, explaining, condemning, redefining and reclaiming meanings of words the mass media has deformed. 'How do you prevent jihadism?' hits back the presenter. K. A says he doesn't understand that word. He describes the 'jihad' he's just done; a personal struggle to get to the studio that evening entailing bus and train hassles. He goes on to reclaim the meaning and separate it from the 'ism' that has been grafted on to it. The presenter repeats the question, redefining their interpretation of the word.

At a red traffic light, I glance in the rear-view mirror at my daughter. 'They're not listening to a thing he says, are they?', she muses. 'Why do they bother asking when they don't care about understanding the answer? It's just rude.' She continues to stare out the window, as her smile slips away somewhere. I want to reach behind, find it and give it back to her.

Should I turn the radio off? I don't, I want to hear the rest. Selfish? Maybe. But she's 18 years old and she's heard worse, I rationalise to myself. What harm can this do? I carry on listening and make a conscious note about my driving. Am I sure all the lights are green when I'm going through? My mind is somewhere else. I try to bypass feelings of guilt for imposing this award-worthy (for its unpleasantness) interview on my daughter, as the interviewer digresses into some parallel discussion about ideologies that I missed the beginning of.

We arrive at the house ten minutes later and I remember I'm a mother. Smile, I tell myself, and wish her well. Younger and faster than me, she switches from the radio wavelength to 'happy-to-meet-friends' mode, anticipating a talking marathon, and her smile returns. She dashes off as my call of '... and make sure you get some sleep!' trails behind her. But her eyes say something else. It's amazing how different parts of our face contradict one another. Her eyes speak of an unsettled feeling, of something unsavoury and foul tasting being swallowed. I turn the car around and head back; the interview continues.

The tone of the questions scorch and it's getting worse. K. A's part is over, and the presenters analyse the witnesses' discussion. One of them, a professor, says K. A hasn't tackled the real problem: that *Iz-lam* is not compatible in a secular world, that the *Kur-aan* needs reforming. 'Until that can be admitted, we're not going to get anywhere', he concluded with a nasal snort and scoff.

This is my faith they're talking about. *This – is – my – faith – my – life,* I hear a voice inside me shout. How did we get here? I feel numb.

The presenters continue their analysis and give Islam, my way of life, a death sentence for the next ten minutes. This is the fifth time this week I've heard or read something negative about my faith from unplanned interactions with the media or school correspondence. Headlines that require deconstructing with our young adults. School letters framed in a troubling narrative about the susceptibility of our children to extremism. Social media threads about the difficulty of defining 'Islamophobia'. All the while the reality of what Islamophobia means as you walk around minding your own business is played out on the streets. A fire is spreading while panels of important people are busy debating whether a lighter or a match is an effective instrument to light a cigarette.

Two weeks ago, I spent a while with both teens unravelling the contents of a school assembly that left them demoralised about how the word 'halal' was interpreted in an assembly about animal rights. Off we went into the pastures about the care and compassion animals are meant to be shown and the true meaning of halal.

I arrive home and recall this is Ramadan and there are things to do before breaking fast. The children and my husband join in with the prep. My husband's sorting out the dates and juices and starts chatting to me about something. I have no idea what he's talking about and make some generic comments that mean nothing to either of us. I'm irritable and don't want to snap at anyone just before breaking fast. And anyway, none of them have caused it, it's the radio presenters.

In the ten minutes left before the *adhān* signals the end of the fast, I sit down where the rest of my family is, and I reach out for my *muṣḥaf*. This Divine and noble book that only an hour ago was so rudely and mockingly relegated to needing updating by a stranger sat in some recording studio. I start to read and Radio Score's presenters' voices ring in my ears; their long-winded 'isms' and 'ists' and complicated phrases swirling around my head. I swallow my tears, taken aback by their arrival. Something hurts. I don't want anyone to notice. My husband closes his *muṣḥaf*, walks past me with a hug to signal it's time to break our fast. He senses enough to comfort me; the details don't matter.

We bite into our Medjoul dates, quench our thirst, offer *ṣalāt al-Maghrib*. We eat our meal, clear up and sit down with our cups of tea and share how the day went. The TV normally stays off during Ramadan. Tonight though, I don't care about maintaining the standards we set all those years back. I want to hear other languages I understand, other languages that, for the time being at least, don't mock.

Flipping from Urdu to Bangla, to Hindi, back to an Urdu channel, the sounds sooth my numbness. Something stirs and I feel warmer. The programmes don't interest me, but the languages do, other phrases, intonations, expressions, constructions. I want my ears to drown in these languages, in all of them at the same time.

I stop at a Punjabi channel and check whether I can understand more now, than years ago. My son comes and sits closer to me, intrigued with what I'm smiling at. I realise I can only decipher half of each sentence, but it makes me smile. It reawakens the chaos and exhilaration of our road trip around India with my parents. Vivid, as though I'd just returned, I remember how we walked across the border from Lahore to Amritsar, then sat on a *tongy* (horse carriage), catching glimpses of the Golden Temple through its open ornate gates. I was twelve years old and hungry to consume as much of India as I could with my eyes and take it back home to England with me forever. Souvenirs were lifeless, one dimensional in comparison.

I flip through the Bangla channels – a domestic scene, a betrayed wife who continues to gaze passively out the window at the dusty, parched tree and the empty rickshaw parked in front of the neighbouring block of flats. But there's no dialogue, the silent reflection lasts too long, until a flashback where the actress ponders on the word: *'bhorosha'*.[59] I flip again, back to another Urdu channel and I am transported to a flood-lit garden, breathing in the fragrant night Jasmine as the protagonist and her hero edge toward professing their love, or regrets, I'll never know as

59 Bengali for 'trust'.

I switch the TV off after *'kaisai yakeen dilaw?'*[60] My ears are satiated. I hush the critical inner voice that tells me I'm being idealistic. *People are derogatory about your faith in those languages too, wake up*, it says.

By now our elder daughter is having an in-depth discussion about the history of Iraq with her father. The sound of their conversation in English reminds me of the radio presenters and irritates me. And I'm frustrated knowing that I'll reach for my journal later tonight and have no choice but to use the same language of derision and scorn to express how it's made me feel. How perverse. But languages are a blessing, I chide myself. Languages are these colossal vehicles carrying the best expressions of our humanity, and the very worst.

For now, I don't want to hear any more English or about the history of any land. Tonight, I have to process my younger daughter's history. The history of her heart that houses her faith – her faith that is regularly a target of mockery on every media platform. What is the real damage of watching, reading and hearing these regular onslaughts? How do I measure the stress they cause? I saw her eyes framed by the rear-view mirror – a mirror I never expected to reflect uncomfortable truths when I learnt to drive. Do our young adults develop resilience and critical mind-sets? Does this exposure strengthen them? I don't have any answers. I have no idea what it's doing to me either – none the wiser for the added years.

Tonight, I have to face our children's histories; the whole generation of them growing up with their ears and eyes, their

60 Urdu for 'How can I make you believe me?'

skin and inhaled breaths infused with this derision in the airwaves. There's much written and spoken about 'identity and belonging', about British values, about the mental health and wellbeing of young people in particular. And the work around these matters. But what happens to our children caught in the middle of contradicting messages? Which ruler do we use to measure the effect on their wellbeing of ridiculing the most important identity they have? How is Radio Score contributing to a sense of belonging?

Time for the night prayers is fast approaching. This is Ramadan, I remind myself. Soon, the best sound for my soul, the recitation of tonight's verses of the Qur'ān, will drown out the sadness. Standing in front of the Lord of the heavens and earth will for sure bring solace no TV channel can. I reflect on how a mother's heart expands to absorb the damage that these experiences cause. And I remind myself that she's most likely to be fine tonight, enjoying a Ramadan evening with her closest friends, and more resilient than me. I'll have to pick this up with her another day, hear her take, talk it through. This is what we do, this is our parenting.

I head off to prepare for prayer, this time of succour.

So, what do you think Saba? It's only a fraction of the experiences we were discussing though. Nothing can capture all sides to this unnamed conundrum of the emotional and psychological load we carry around. Thanks for reading it and I look forward to seeing you next week!

All the best with the module readings,
Farida

27

Dear Mother
Searching for a Match for Her Daughter

From:
Another mother at another wedding
In every continent
Every month, every week
Every heartbeat
Since the search started.

As-salāmu ʿalaykum,

You and I don't know each other but here we are, random guests, thrown together in this milieu of excitement. New beginnings, chiffons, silks, sequins and net, sweeping across our table laden with white crockery. Our swift introduction to each other included the usual questions about who we know here, the groom's side or the bride's? It's amusing that we're both here as mothers of the bride and groom's friends! Our exchange was enough to register the similar predicament we're in. We didn't need to say anymore.

I see your pensive expression return between the smile filled greetings and rendezvous with past acquaintances and *that* relative of yours you held a conversation with, awkwardly. To your credit, you managed it.

The 'trying not to look contemplative' expression is one I recognise as easily as my own reflection, having worn it so often, particularly in public like today. This is what many of us, mothers, do who are mentally exhausted from searching for that one person for our son or daughter. Just the one. One human being. And here we are surrounded by scores of 'eligible' boys and 'eligible' girls and yet no closer to the one we're earnestly looking for. Maybe looking for a son is easier, time will tell.

Looking. Seeing. Listening. Reflecting. Evaluating. Assessing. Reading. Replying. Moving on to the next one. On loop. This loop has grown into a ride my life is locked into. I search to find the 'stop' button and find the exit. I didn't queue to get on this ride. I set off to do a parent's duty, an act rooted in faith and love, to help them start their next stage of life. A step taken when there were no signs of it happening by itself.

These past years have given the word 'looking' a new meaning, haven't they? It started with our eyes when life was simple, and we believed naively that 'looking' for a match was as simple as blinking.

Then it moved on to another level when we realised 'looking' is something that defies twenty-twenty vision, something where perspective and seeing are not neatly aligned with perception and settling.

'Looking', then mutated into the more desperate relative – 'searching'. Then 'searching' morphed into 'seeking' in that low-lying, full-time, invisible, painfully private yet public occupation we mothers have. It wouldn't be so bad if we were left to our private sorrow of answering inane questions knowing they are not going to go anywhere; of following up bios (who even thought up these categories: 'eye colour', 'celebrates milaads & Khatams', 'caste'?).

Maybe it wouldn't be so bad if the conversations didn't feel as though you are talking about the merits of installing an air conditioning unit in the north pole. *This is your daughter – not a product you are marketing* – the voice of reason reminds you. You shake yourself mentally out of the shackles of this loop for a few days to regain your life.

It looks like you've avoided what we mothers dread this evening: the unexpected public address of our 'searching status' from well-wishers. You are brave, you're interacting. I've chosen not to this evening. I observe from the sidelines, comfortable with watching the crimson sky fade into paler shades as the sun sets around this banqueting suite.

The 'searching status' questions are normally followed with advice. I know we've all done it ourselves too. Well-meaning advice. Well-intentioned advice. Well-targeted advice like having one's ear pierced: 'You're looking in the wrong places sister. Have you tried...', or 'You need to lower your standards, education's not everything. Would you consider...', or the best one of all, 'Well, if you'd started earlier, then...', as though, like queuing up for Next Sale at 5am, it would guarantee finding the right catch for your daughter. Or like a fisherman going out in the depths of the night before the others to make sure his bait tempts the right fish. I've had to face all of these and a dozen more.

The awfulness of the language around finding a life-partner for a son or daughter is almost as dreadful as the regular interactions with the wrong candidates. The language is actually worse for someone with a keen ear looking for harmony between this process we're in and the subtle, beautiful Qur'ānic metaphors of *zawj* (a partner) or *libās* (a garment). It's as though all the current 'matchmaking' language needs to be banned, deleted, abolished and replaced with a new dialect that is intelligent and honest. Take the common 'halal dating' site adverts, does this oxymoron not even bother anyone? Those ten-line profiles crammed onto a phone screen are actually spiritual beings with a heart, soul, mind and personalities. They deserve more than the narrow categories better suited to describing a crate of objects.

This state of searching – full of contradictions, void of substance – this is where we exist in this parallel universe of being a parent. The fact that there have been hundreds and thousands of parents around the globe, going back centuries and across cultures, doing this doesn't seem to have helped what we are experiencing now.

When did it go so wrong? How and where? Is it the mix of the many different backgrounds and ideas that has caused the confusion in people's minds about what to prioritise? The inner verses the outer, faith verses education, forefathers' roots verses current family location, job level verses social status. We are stuck in binaries and tangled. We collectively need to reshape this, starting with the conversations we have.

How do you find the conversation develop when 'faith' or 'practice' are mentioned? In the beginning I found a huge spectrum; for some parents or young men, being 'religious' was an outdated accessory and wholly irrelevant. Then I got experienced and only looked into profiles where faith sounded like it was part of that person's life. Naturally, with that then comes the second step of how 'Muslim' is translated in their life. My aunt commented in exasperation one day: 'We'd never heard of so many types of Muslims in our time. Either you were Muslim or Hindu, *bass*. What is this now!'

Our problems are universal, I guess that's some consolation for you and me. We are certainly not alone. Out there, somewhere in the galaxy, we seek clusters of light to find our way ahead. These galaxies witnessed the journeys of our foremothers wearing the same pensive look we wear – for different reasons, but they wore it too. Our search, their search and the millions in between us stretch far out beyond the boundaries of land and sea. Beyond the flags of nationality and continent, beyond the lineage of tribes and the migration of grandparents. Beyond his age and her height, our journey together exists in its own stratosphere.

You sit down and you are taking a view from the side-lines now too. There's much to absorb in the youthful milieu of flamboyant enthusiasm and hope as the brocade fabrics pass by the monochrome suits. I feel your need to rest these uncertain footsteps on this unpredictable terrain. When did we get here?

There was a time when it was safe to dream and joke, laugh and paint entertaining scenes with friends about weddings that might happen, could happen, would of course, *in shā' Allāh*, happen. And then the years rolled those carefree thoughts up in a rug and ran away when we weren't looking.

What remained was the concrete reality of our children reaching a 'stage' where they are ready to move on with their own lives as one half of a whole: as that *zawj*. We too moved our parenting up a gear to prepare for this stage. We got ready and waited. And waited. When matches didn't fall out from the sky or sprout organically from the ground, we realised it was time to roll up our sleeves and help.

This is how we got here. This is how we ended up with the expressions that surface from beneath the layers of under-eye gel, anti-wrinkle cream, serum, foundation, concealer and face powder. All of it useless compared to the tales our eyes tell.

People will debate and criticise, advise, and opine against looking for suitable matches for our children. 'Times have changed', they'll say, 'leave it to them', 'why are you bothered, it's not your problem', 'who wants a parent finding a match anyway – not in today's day and age.' Opinions and unsolicited opinions will flow like water. For so many reasons that neither you nor I need to explain, the reality stands today that we, their mothers, are helping them with this stage of life. On top of the difficulties we're facing, it would help not having to justify supporting our son or daughter's quest to complete half their faith.

At least you and I made it out here tonight. Not everyone does. Some mothers retreat quietly. They gradually withdraw from social settings to limit their struggle and protect what's left of their minds. For some, it all gets too much. I'm not surprised when I think about the stages of menopause too amidst all of this. It's not difficult to figure out that many of us, having these stressful matchmaking conversations, are either pre-menopausal or actually dealing with this physiological change which affects everything about us till things settle down. No one wants to acknowledge this though, but I will!

When I'm less emotional and take a step back, it helps me to remember that Our Creator says, '*Every human We created experiences hardship.*'[61] The angst and confusion are replaced by some clarity; that this is a test where we can try our best, along with accepting that the ultimate result is out of our hands. Our role, as parents, is as much about trusting in our *du'ā's* and returning to these no matter what. Trusting that *al-Laṭīf*, The Subtle, Who is aware of every emotion we go through, will answer our *du'ā's*. *Du'ā's* are answered, and we have to stay firm in returning to this reality. *Du'ā's* are our lifeline.

And when we step back, we recognise in time that there is a better plan, far better than our limited vision can see. It's not only the literal 'prick of a thorn' that the believer is compensated for.[62] Our shortcomings are erased for all types of hardship like worry and stress, if we remain patient and constant.

I hope sharing our journey may bring some form of comfort. There are so many more sides to this I didn't mention today, like the layers of discomfort we see in our son's or daughter's eyes and shy away from. That's for another day.

For this evening I'll stop here. I've run out of paper on my mini paper pad that goes everywhere with me. Just as well, as I've turned a corner having shared my thoughts with you and now feel ready to be part of this delightful

---

61 *Sūrah al-Balad* 90: 4.
62 The Prophet (ﷺ) said: "No fatigue, illness, anxiety, sorrow, harm or sadness afflicts any Muslim, even to the extent of a thorn pricking him, without Allah wiping out his sins by it." *Ṣaḥīḥ al-Bukhārī.*

occasion of new beginnings. Here and now, there is joy to participate in.

We will start again too, pick up where we left off, with an open heart to find that one match.

Bismillāh.

Your sister in searching

28

DEAR MOTHER
OF AN 'EMPTY NEST'

From:
Rafiqa
Your once teenage friend
Now ripe accomplice
Spreading my wings
At the tree-top with a bird's eye view

Jamila, dearest Jamila!

Thank you for your last letter announcing the huge milestone of Hashim settling into his new job in the South of the island. We knew he'd be the brave one venturing into new pastures; good for him! It sounds like adventures await him and his wife in that scenic area!

And it was a joy to read about how well the girls are doing, building their lives around their fledgling families. Their hurdles you described reminded me of our early days and all the 'unknowns' that accompanied every pot of tea we shared.

Remember all that stress, weighing up the pros and cons of the local primary school or home school, Montessori or Islamic schools? Which catchment area for Secondary schools? Which weekend supplementary school or madrasah system to go for, or whether we just do it ourselves? Finding a reliable Arabic teacher was another mission after the spectrum we discovered!

As if we didn't have our hands full already, we managed, with some raw determination, to juggle our small businesses and sign up for courses too. One way or another, it happened. Some years passed at their own pace. Other years sped by with no time for anything to register. Races around the domestic and school circuit to the next birthday, the next parents' evening, the next Ramadan, the next exams and assignments, to the next Eid. They became blurred milestones with no finish line. I feel tired seeing it on paper now, how were we living it? After all these stages you're now finally joining me at the 'empty nest' stage. The best I can do during a pandemic is to share your 'coming of stage' through this letter, and sadly not yet in person.

I've had to think more about this stage of life since Sonia got married two years ago. It took a while for both of us parents to adjust; fathers find it tough in different ways. Remember how worried I was, especially as the three of us were a small family already? I had to look at the whole thing differently; to see it as our family expanding and gaining a new member. As simple as it sounds, it took a while to really believe this. But eventually that mind-set helped so much, expanding rather than contracting our world.

It's a wonderful cycle of life to see them thriving, reminding us of those early years of married life. When I moved much further away, it would have been emotionally tough if my parents were constantly sad, or lonely. But thankfully they didn't have much time for that with my four younger siblings at home. In this new stage, I've gotten used to a pattern in our life and relish our time together while no longer pining our daughter's presence.

It's unfortunate that there's a negative tone when people refer to this stage of life. In the last couple of years, I've come to realise that witnessing our children marry and settle is a privilege, as we know quite a few who weren't given life long enough to see this. To have our life span encompass seeing our adult children's lives develop, is a huge blessing. Strong wings and a certain sense of direction takes them places we may not have ventured; they're out on their own flight, and the days of us managing it all are done.

Do you remember how we questioned what we were doing, all that soul searching, wondering if we were helping or inhibiting, strengthening or stifling? Thank God for everything turning out alright through the hurdles we faced. Even though we both had differences in the number of children we were handling and their specific ups and downs, it was a life support to have our few friends and relatives to share it with. It took us a while till we realised the results of our efforts are out of our hands, and it's the huge mercy of God that kept them safe and their hearts guided.

And now, off they've flown. Where does that leave you and me; mothers who've spent our lives putting our children first? Do we feel lost when we shut the front door after they leave, not recognising who it is left standing in our hallway? Who is 'she' now? Is it parenting that changes us, or time that births new versions of us? Having been through it now, I'd say embrace this stage, Jamila. I'll admit I gradually grew to love the newfound space I found myself standing in, and I don't feel guilty in saying that either!

Space – yes! Mental space to think. Space to look inside and figure out: what next? Where next? And how do I *do* the 'next'? It doesn't mean anything drastic like a bucket list of world locations to tick off. But these questions are what I asked myself to get things clear in my head over the following months. All these years we've known each other, our heads were usually taken up with one phase or problem to overcome, or another. Even when they got older, remember how we felt helpless about some of their choices, and on edge as to what we would face next? Parents feel vulnerable too, we learnt. Parents can be powerless, too, we saw. We got through it, Jamila, by the grace of God. And now I'm savouring this time to think about the greater purpose of the time we have left here.

You know how I've had health issues over the years. Thankfully, I had good health around the time of Sonia's wedding, and I remember feeling relieved not to be battling any symptoms. Each day was a conscious realisation. I remember thinking, 'I'm not ill – thank God.' Since she's left, that perspective's continued, so on good days, I'm grateful I've got the whole day to invest in things apart from symptom control. That's how I started to look at this new 'space' positively.

Just like you, I'm a 'list person', so I made a list of what I'd done over the years, things I enjoyed which I could do something useful with. That was my first step into loving this new stage of life. It took a few weeks to figure it all out, but it was well worth it. Seeing the needs in my local community written down, alongside the experience I had, helped me think ahead.

I also love how streams of time can now flow into the extended family and friends further afield; there's a whole support system there, where youngsters and elders alike welcome the company, or help. Before this stage, there was always too many of my own household's commitments to see to. And you know what, having some time for us as a couple, not just as 'Mother & Father management team', was a welcome adjustment too!

One of the best things I did in the beginning was to have a regular day, every fortnight where I spend time with my uncle and aunt, rather than the ad hoc way I used to see them. We make plans, and it's good to have this time together regularly. My uncle's expressions are so similar to my mother's, it comforts me seeing him and his wife. And they look forward to our day together so eagerly. The other thing that gives my week structure is volunteering with the women's group at the food bank. It's been just perfect for doing something together. Last year, fundraising with them was my first experience of this sort of thing and I loved it. I think I've reconnected with who '*she*', standing at the door, is now. Any more than this and my health issues would get in the way, but this much I can manage.

Jamila, I'd describe this stage as a reservoir – it's what we look for that matters. What we find doesn't need to be grand or exciting, just whatever has meaning for you. That family history you wanted to record, the batik printing you wanted to learn – that's just a couple of things I've dug up from my memory! You wanted to spend more time with your parents and cousins – there's finally time to make more plans now.

You mentioned in your letter that you're finding it 'hard to let go'. That's you, me and everyone else from the beginning of time I expect. I'll bet every mother feels she's the only one going through this. But it's a reality that this separation is the way of the world, the most natural cycle that we've been through ourselves! Since you mentioned it, I've been thinking how for some parents there's more to it. Sometimes their holding on can get out of balance, to fill a void.

I found it took me a while to find the middle ground between this pendulum of holding on and letting go that swings in our maternal head. How do I describe it? At times it felt as though 'letting go' was like sitting in an audience seat at the theatre, watching your child's life story unfold. Watching Act I move into Act II from a distance. Sat there, you watch them transform as they grow through life's experiences. Will they walk tall with a strong spine, or do they lose their balance? The invisible ties of the womb tug and make you want to leave your seat and intervene. But you don't move. You watch them figure their steps out themselves.

Other times your support *is* necessary – you leave your seat and step forward to assist. By this time, you've got used to this new normal. I understand how you're feeling now though, as it's early days for you. And as hard as it is, you hit on such a sensitive point in your letter – discussing that alone could have been my whole letter. I hope you don't mind me quoting that bit you wrote:

And how are we meant to feel about the selfless affection and care we gave from their birth, when they've gone and it's not reciprocated? Is this how it works? I know we weren't perfect (far from it) but we just knew that our parents deserved our time and attention, after marriage without actually thinking it through. We did what we could. I don't know if I'm making sense Rafiqa – it's more like they calculate how much attention to give us. Whatever you call this, it hurts.

There's too much to say on this for this letter, we'll talk about it on a call. It's early days Jamila, you're all adjusting. What might look like them not reciprocating is part of their readjusting to a new life in a new place too – but we will talk about it soon!

All I can say is, you carry on with your resourceful, purposeful presence on this earth. Savour fewer demands on your time, it might be short-lived. Thankfully your parents are both in good health, so you're fortunate to spend time with them regularly. But we never know with our parents' health (or our own) what tomorrow can bring. This is a time we can invest in leaving a legacy, public or private, large scale or modest, there's no prescription. It takes some work, but if we can align our intentions and what we do with ourselves, we'll find our own way of seeing this stage with hope and joy. Sure, I know, there's a dozen steps between each of these!

And finally, I've also realised our 'work' and role as mothers doesn't stop just because our children, or in my case our only child, has a new address and is building a new life. Our invisible work as mothers continue. More like a fragrance than a physical presence, our role permeates their lives in new unnamed ways. We still need each other.

I'm living in hope that these Covid travel ban restrictions will be lifted once it's safe enough, *in shā' Allāh*, and then we can finally meet up and enjoy some of this time together – this stage of an 'expanding nest'!

Much love as always,
Rafiqa

29

DEAR MOTHER
WHO IS MY GRAND-DAUGHTER

From:
Dadu
Your paternal home
Carrying generations of ancestral wisdom

My dearest Lateefah,

This is the greatest delight I could hope for in this world, seeing you as a mother – all gratitude to Allah (ﷻ) for it. The memory of your last visit with the children keeps me warm inside, a scene I replay every time I want to feel joy.

I write to you with a heart full of delight and gratitude. It's been too long since the last letter, I know. A *Dadu* usually hands over Rajshahi silk sarees and hand painted China tea sets, occasional furniture pieces or a Cadbury tin of photos to their grandchildren.[63] Your *Dadu* writes you letters (yes, I have also kept the porcelain dish you have had your eye on aside for you!). After the last letter about our family traditions, today I have a different subject for you: values. While the last letter had colourful descriptions of rituals, keepsakes, recipes and special occasions, none of it would have been inherited were it not for the values that stitch them all together. Let me explain ...

Values are usually brushed over. As they're abstract, they're not the easiest topic to digest. If people do broach the subject of 'family values' for instance, they tend to mean something different to each family. Take 'success' as a value; what is success for one person may be doom and gloom for

_____
63 *Dadu* means paternal grandmother in Bangla.

another. What I think is a big challenge for your generation is the speed at which values are changing. I wonder how you will fare concerning the ideas about family and society, the fads and fashions about raising children, the beliefs about marriage and the roles of each *zawj* (spouse, companion and partner – this is a much more beautiful term than husband and wife). I think about this often. I wasn't sure how to write to you about this subject, so I'll start from what I know best: my past.

I became a mother in a different land, which belonged to a different world. A world where the radio and newspapers were the only external voices that entered our lives. At times, even those felt like one too many when the novelty of the air waves wore off. There were plenty of *real* voices around us all day and night, too many sometimes!

I was surrounded by women in so many situations, tested by the world and its web of relationships. Some soldiered through, managing their homes and social work; they were the locally born leaders. Others quietly worked through their problems, occupied with survival. Our lives, the silk weft and warp yarns criss-crossing one another, built the fabric of the community. Other women, like my mother and two of my elder sisters were the 'architects'; they built the framework of the extended family, connecting people together, mending whatever broke, keeping things moving.

This is the setting in which we became mothers. The 'we' included neighbours, sisters and cousins. We became mothers in stages, leaves budding on the same tree. Much of the time, we thought together. Individual choices were limited to the brazen ones who dared to think or live on their own terms. Some of the matriarchs were forward thinking and open to change; some were working in roles outside the home, in schools and universities, in the medical field and charities. Even with this variety, the branches were firm, and we were all connected in some way.

When it came to getting married and having our own family, we looked up at our elders and across at our peers; a colourful array with examples of good marriages and unfortunately ample examples of injustice and tragedy too. There was enough going on in front of our eyes to keep us alert and humble.

Why am I sharing this with you, my Lateefa? It's to show you there were frictions and difficulties in our time too, before and during motherhood. Through those problems though, the one thing that bound us together were our values: certain gold standards – the *zari* motif running through our community. No matter how the shape of the motifs differed between family to family, they were still woven from the same *zari* threads.

Values are timeless. Time moves us on to new places, new ways of living and thinking. Certain values, though, when raising a family, need to be protected through the social storms and new versions of 'normal' that will appear. Values such as honesty, no matter if you face embarrassment from it; integrity, that your thoughts and actions are aligned; trustworthiness, that you are reliable to your family and community; compassion and humility; forgiveness and sacrifice are a few of the motifs that should stay in fashion, no matter where we go or which era we live in. Building a family depends on both the husband and wife upholding certain principles.

This brings me to the beliefs we hold about being mothers. Our role as mothers (yes, there are many more sides to a woman, as we've discussed often) should be secure, without confusion. The world will throw up contradictions, we will be tested over and over, but your 'role' need not be bewildering, my warm-hearted granddaughter. I hear the opinions about the position of a woman, about being a mother, about even having a womb within our bodies (this was debated on a TV chat show I watched). Protect yourself from this confusion my dear – be clear in your mind that your womb is not an accident of nature, or a curse, or – what did they call it? – a 'sociological construction' that you need to challenge in order to assert your rights and your existence. As we ponder on Our *Rabb*'s blessed names and attributes, *al-Asmā' wa'l-Ṣifāt*, our understanding of His creation strengthens.[64]

That women are different to men is a blessing. That we are designed to be unique in our nature is a sign of His Magnificence. I know you are well versed in Islam's equity between the sexes, so I need not say anything more on this point. The tragedy is not our *Dīn* that causes confusion about our nature and roles, but people. Either they are ignorant of the sacred teachings of Islam or intent on misinterpreting them.

Our *fiṭrah* (innate nature) is a powerful thing, an intriguing thing. When a person understands that Allah (﷾) put our nature into us which is what makes us human, then there's less chance of being swayed every time ideas

64 The Names and Attributes of Allah (﷾).

that are opposed to the *fiṭrah* are unleashed on society. One day the opinions about parents' roles blow south, the next day they rage northwards and mothers are expected to sway with each change of direction. So, our values need anchoring. God gave you a mind to think about what you see and hear. When you hear 'new' ideas about the nature of women, about the place of marriage and motherhood in society, ask yourself how aligned these are to the *fiṭrah* we have within us? This *āyah* stands out in my mind about this:

> *So stand firmly for the religion of Allah sincerely. This is the human nature which Allah made. There is no change in the laws of Allah's creation. This is the upright religion, most people don't know.*[65]

And yes, Lateefa, we challenge injustices done to women. Yes, we do our best to change the status quo when it's oppressive to mothers. But we don't need to confuse this with thinking her constitution is deficient. Remember when my niece (your aunt) had to divorce. Nobody said it was wrong, because every avenue of helping the couple had been exhausted. Trust and respect between this couple was in shreds. Instead, we supported her and her children. It took both parents time to move on, but they did, not trying to change the meaning of what a mother and father is. They got on with their individual roles because that was never the issue in the first place.

Which leads me to the subject of men, as husbands and fathers. Men, like your committed and thoughtful husband are partners in life's journey to the Hereafter. The *zawj* is a confidante, helper, supporter, protector, advisor

65 *Sūrah al-Rūm* 30: 30.

when he is fulfilling his role. Men and women are a team. Team members are not competitors in a marriage, and as parents that team needs to be solid as its strength will be tested again and again. Why does it sound like nowadays respecting men is a sign of weakness or subjugation? Don't people in a family respect each other as a long-held value?

Women from my generation had healthy marriages too – it wasn't all the doom that is commonly talked about. They loved and were loved by equitable men: their fathers and brothers and husbands. Not all of human existence is a sorry saga of inequalities. I've lived through many moons to see this for myself. As for the unacceptable, oppressive patriarchy that poisoned large sections of the community back then, this has still sadly persisted in today's world and it's frustrating to see old cycles continue.

There were voices going back in our history who publicly challenged the patriarchy of the time they lived in, and privately there were many more who worked quietly, determined to challenge the inequities. My mother and *Nani Amma* used to mention the figure of Begum Rokeya Sakhawat, a social activist who had an impact on the women of Bengal. She raised her voice about the injustices caused by oppressive patriarchy.[66] I have one of her collected works translated and want to share an extract from it with you:

Anyway, the purpose of education is not to blindly imitate a community or a race. It is to develop the innate faculties of the individual, attributed by God, through cultivation. Proper use of these qualities is

66 Rokeya Sakhawat Hossain, *Woman's Downfall*, trans by Mohammad A. Quayum, *Transnational Literature*, Vol 4, no 1, November 2011.

incumbent upon us, and their dissipation is a vice. God has given us hands, legs, eyes, ears, imagination and the power to think. If we strengthen our hands and legs through exercise, do good deeds with our hands, observe attentively with our eyes, listen carefully with our ears, and learn to make our thinking ability more sophisticated through reflection, then that is true education. We do not consider the pursuit of academic degrees as real education. Let me give you an example of the flowering and enhancement of visual powers.

A scientifically trained eye sees charming and beauteous objects where an untrained eye sees only clay and dust. The earth that we trample on with contempt, taking it as mere soil, mud, sand and coal dust – scientists will, on analysis, find there four kinds of valuable items. For example, cultured sand results in opal; modified clay can be used in making porcelain or sapphire; and processed coal can make diamond. From water we get vapour and mist. So you see, sisters. Where an illiterate eye sees clay, an enlightened eye sees ruby and diamond. We keep such priceless eyes forever blind; how will we answer for it to God?'[67]

Look where I've taken you – all the way back to the early 1900s! The point is, injustices were tackled, but core values about womanhood were retained. The oppression was challenged, not the very existence of being a woman.

---

67 Rokeya Sakhawat Hossain, *Woman's Downfall*, trans by Mohammad A. Quayum, *Transnational Literature*, Vol 4, no 1, November 2011.p.13

So, I come back to the point – that in all the stages you go through hold on to the balanced, middle way. Sometimes, people abandon the middle way as a reaction to injustices. They lose sight of the Divinely inspired framework which is wide and flexible enough to apply to all different times and places. We people have block printed a narrow picture of what a balanced role looks like.

Did I tell you about the lady I met in *al-Masjid al-Nabawī* on my last *'Umrah* trip? She was employed as one of the team caring for the upkeep of the *masjid*. She came from India to do this job, going back to visit her family once every two years. Back in her hometown, she left grown children who were raised by her mother and sister. Her husband, she explained sadly, had fallen ill and was subsequently paralysed and in need of regular medication. After trying her best to find work locally and not succeeding, she saw the advert to come to Madinah and work in the *masjid*. 'This is the most beloved occupation to me on earth,' she said with such contentment. She supported her family and managed her husband's medical treatment with her income. Her warm, uninhibited smile when she told me she's going back for her daughter's wedding this year will stay with me. Whatever the rights and wrongs of her situation, the point is: there is breadth and flexibility in how we manage our families and roles because no two families on this earth are the same. With compassion and commitment difficulties are overcome.

If people abuse their rights and neglect their responsibilities, then they are at fault, not the guidance we have. When you weave a home together in a pattern aligned to what Allah (ﷻ) ordained, that thread won't falter. It will embellish whatever material – your *rizq* (sustenance) – is given to you. Be conscious of our *Rabb's* norms and it will save you from much confusion. Ask yourself when you see imbalances: which ideas and reference points are causing it? More often than not, you'll find the balance in Our Sustainer's guidance has been abandoned and something experimental has replaced it.

On this middle path, raising children doesn't need to be your sole project or badge of honour with every waking moment focused on them alone; they will have unrealistic expectations of you. Nor should they be treated like an inconvenience; they will be the first to know they are not cherished but tolerated. Every *Jumu'ah* when we read *Sūrah al-Kahf*, the clear reminder helps us to keep our priorities in order, affirming that: '*Wealth and children are beautiful decorations of this life. However, the fruit of good deeds will remain with your Lord, an excellent reward and hope.*'[68]

Part of maintaining this middle ground is the expectations we, mothers, have. Too many expectations on ourselves and we end up resentful with the 'must do' list becoming overwhelming. Too few reasonable expectations, and the slightest inconvenience and discomfort becomes unbearable, and the honoured role feels like a punishment. I remember seeing this problem with expectations playing out right in front of my teenage eyes, all those years ago. It's something I only understood many years later.

Minu Apa, was what we called her. She and her husband with their young child moved in as tenants in one of the flats

---

68 *Sūrah al-Kahf* 18: 46.

beside our house. I had just finished my IA exams, along with a couple of cousins and friends in the same batch. We were around 18 years old and idle for a few weeks. We'd pass time sitting on the roof top in the evenings. That's when we'd hear Minu Apa's lyrical sobs. How she hated her life, and didn't understand her fastidious, boring husband. How she disliked where they lived (it was a poor neighbourhood compared to her parents' home). How she despised the fabric he bought her and how she never wanted any of this – the labour of caring for their child all day long without help, and ... and ... so it would continue. She was destined for greatness, *'bikhyato hobo'* (I will be famous), she snapped. Followed by the declaration that there was nothing even vaguely grand in their life, 'My life with you is like being trapped in a mosquito net!' She lamented her separation from the whole world, the world deprived of her talents.

Her *nokhshi kathas* were the boldest, most exquisitely embroidered we'd seen; orange and red threads on an indigo background.[69] They were left out to air, besides beaded chiffon sarees draped on the washing line; a dramatic display. Were these clues to her grandeur, we wondered. And what would she like to tell the world, that the rural women's needles hadn't already communicated?

We'd crouch low to sneak a look at any talents and greatness visible when she was pacing along the veranda, her hair skilfully pinned into a perfect beehive. Some evenings we only heard their short arguments, a ping pong match of dissatisfaction. But on other evenings a chorus of

69 Traditional hand embroidered cotton layered quilts of Bengali origin.

complaints were sung between the sobs. When their radio was on, the sounds got confused, and we couldn't tell if it was her monologue or the chorus of a folk song that we were listening to.

Was it a bad match we wondered? Did she want to marry someone else, or maybe not marry at all? Or perhaps she'd run away to marry him and then grew discontent with the reality of daily life. Was looking after the child too much for her; didn't she love her daughter? Or was he to blame? Maybe he never took her to nice places, we theorised, as we shelled nuts and tossed them into our mouths.

I don't know what happened to Minu Apa. We heard she went to stay with her *khālah* in Savar one Eid and never returned. After a couple of months, new tenants moved in and our term at college began. We forgot about the woeful *ghazals* we heard from the rooftop. We forgot their sad episodes, until the Economics Sir turned around from the book cupboard in our first class: it was him – yes, him, Minu Apa's husband – he was our Sir! We hid our surprise of course. Looking back, I see how naive our understanding was. But I've always remembered Minu Apa and wondered when the river grew between the two banks of reality and fantasy. Had she never seen normal married life, we wondered. Perhaps she had, but didn't want that for herself.

There is no one syllabus for married life and motherhood. You make your syllabus as you go along, as your exam is bespoke to your family. There will be overlaps with others, and it helps to share notes on those. Your homes are different universes, so release yourself from the pressures of comparing the minor details and hold on to the golden motifs of our values. Don't let these values die the same death as our finest hand-woven *jamdani* did.[70] It was replaced by cheaper yarn from Europe and industrial manufacturing. There I go again, finding some way to bring up my beloved subject of saree production! You understand what I'm saying though, Lateefa.

For today I will end here. I want to hear your thoughts on all this, if not soon in person, then write them and I can enjoy your thoughts over and over again through your pen.

With my loving *du ʿāʾs* for you all,
Your *Dadu*

70 A fine patterned muslin textile woven in Bangladesh.

30

DEAR DAUGHTER WHO'S JUST GIVEN BIRTH

From:
Amma
In the maternity ward
Seeing your daughter
As a mother
For the first time

Dearest Abeer,

Here I am standing in awe, absorbing the sight of the baby once in my arms now holding *her own* baby in her arms. I am in awe of the cycle of life, the circle of seasons and the ways our lives rotate. Infant turned young child, turned teenager, turned young woman, turned wife, now progressed into being a mother.

It feels as though the world is revolving on an altered axis, a new timeline, showing me a delightful new perspective.

All at once the universe seems to have expanded and gathered all that is good within it to bring you the gift of motherhood and all at once the universe seems to have shrunk and I see the silky wisp of your hair and the tightly clenched small palms, return, brand new, in this new soul you cradle.

A sea of gratitude sweeps over any thoughts or emotions. Undulating gratitude for what is beyond our power, the creation of a new being – a unique being, with thousands of cells and nerves all inter-connected. Cycles and circles spinning out the invisible threads of lineage over time to create the scene before my eyes.

Allāhu Akbar – God is the greatest!

Khayr al-Rāḥimīn – the Best of all those who show mercy![71]

Khayr al-Rāziqīn – the Best of Providers![72]

Alḥamdullilāh – Praise be to Allah!

In these cycles I am reminded of the powerful sign of Allah's (ﷻ) creation and magnificence; of His magnanimous giving to us. Is there anything more miraculous than the birth of a new life – anything more elevated than carrying the decision of the Almighty to bring a new human into existence within our wombs? Is there any closer connection to the reality of His Magnificence than this? What is there beyond gratitude? I ask myself as I absorb this sight.

We are at home now. You are asleep next to your new-born, already completely surrendered to your baby daughter's power to turn night into day and day into night. Surrendered to sustaining her when she's thirsty and checking if she's breathing when her sleep becomes that bit deeper. I would love to bottle these moments: the sweetness of the baby's scent, the blessed feeling that spreads in the home. I always knew you would be a tender mother, ready to embrace this blessing with all the warmth that comes naturally to you.

I ponder the responsibility in your arms, the way I did when I held you. While the physical reality of a baby will

---

71 *Sūrah al Mu'min* 23: 109.
72 *Sūrah al Mā'idah* 5: 114.

overhaul your calendar, the invisible part of the *amānah* of her soul is the heavier of the responsibilities you'll handle. Though unseen, her soul's significance is like the scent of the rarest *oudh* on earth; invisible to our eyes, yet present and priceless. And the challenge lies in nurturing this soul. It is a privilege, a test, a responsibility. A connection with your eternity and theirs.

This baby sleeping beside you will grow and thrive *in shā' Allāh* in their own good time. Your life will be rewired by them expertly. She will bring a whole new circuit into existence to test out your agility, stamina, calmness, reactions, management and internal resources. It is hard to imagine how a small, fragile baby can grow into a whole world of habits and personality, but she will, just like you have.

This stage, as much as it is wrapped in joy and gratitude and a sense of wonder, can at times feel so different to your existence before your baby arrived. It can feel like you have to relearn your way of living, retrieving what you can from the pre-baby days while embracing the presence of your child. All I would advise is don't rush this stage or feel like there's a template you must squeeze yourself and this little one into.

There are daily living needs and boundaries already. These are enough of a cast you'll be pouring your hours and days into, discovering the new shape that emerges. Don't compare to anyone else's pattern either. Do reach out for support, we are here for you. In some languages, there is no word for 'grandparent' they are known by the same word used for 'mother' – there's a good reason for this.

I have faith you will grow into the role of motherhood with sincerity and *iḥsān, in shā' Allāh*. Excellence isn't about the results, or the photos, or any other measure people use. It isn't the popular image of being a 'martyr', as our minds and bodies have rights over us. *Iḥsān* in motherhood is doing the best with the responsibilities you have to discharge in the most equitable, kind way, conscious of our *Rabb* and Sustainer's standards.

I also know you will be challenged – as that is the push and pull of this *dunyā*. It is the struggle we were all born to tackle en route to our eternal home. There is no escaping this struggle. For this period of mothering keep the value of your role at the forefront of your mind. The One we will stand in front of values it highly. Seeing you with your own baby, my heart speaks a language of gratitude beyond the confines of these words. And so, with that, my *du'ā'* for you is:

That you find contentment as a mother.

That you find much joy and happiness and wonder as you go through infancy and childhood with your own child.

That you discover the sweetness of a child's fiṭrah in a million beautiful ways.

That you are blessed with the wisdom, courage and patience to meet the challenges that will come your way, as they do with raising any human being.

That at every turn of life you're blessed with protection from The Protecting Friend.

That our grandchild is a means of reward during your earthly life and in the next.

Āmīn.

With love,
Your proud and grateful *Amma.*

GLOSSARY

Aḥkām – Rulings around an act of worship.

Amānah – A trust.

Āyah – A sign/a 'verse' of the Qur'ān.

Afartan bax – A celebration of 40 days after childbirth.

Barakah – Divine blessings, increase.

Chand raat – Moonlit night.

Daee – Traditional midwife/aid in Bangladesh.

Fiṭrah – The natural disposition of a person.

Ḥalaqah – Teaching and learning circle.

Ḥayā' – Modesty.

Iḥsān – Striving for excellence.

Khālah – Maternal aunt.

Khaṭīb – One who delivers the Friday sermon.

Maqmad – Somali dried meat dish.

M'semmen – Moroccon traditional flatbread.

Muḥtasib – Market inspector.

Libās – Garments or clothes.

Qablah – Midwife in rural areas of Morocco.

Rfissah – Moroccon chicken and lentil dish.

Rizq – Provision.

*Shuk*r – Gratitude.

Taqwā – God consciousness.

Ṭayyib – Pure, wholesome.

Tawwakul – Trusting in Allah.

BIBLIOGRAPHY

Abdel-Halim, Rabie El-Said, 'The Role of Ibn Sina's Medical
    Poem in the Transmission of Medical Knowledge to Medieval
    Europe', *Urology Annals*, Vol 6, Issue 1, Jan–Mar 2014, pp. 1–12,
    doi: 10.4103/0974-7796.127010.

Abu Zayd al-Balkhi, *Sustenance of the Soul: The Cognitive Behaviour
    Therapy of a Ninth Century Physician*, trans by Malik Badri
    (Herndon, The International Institute of Islamic Thought,
    2013).

Allama Iqbal, *Reason and Heart from Bang-e-Dra in The Poetry
    of Allama Iqbal*, trans by Dr Muntasir Mir, ©The Iqbal
    Academy Government of Pakistan http://www.allamaiqbal.
    com/poetry.php?bookbup=22&orderno=15&lang_
    code=en&lang=2&conType=en.

Allama Iqbal, *The Poetry of Allama Iqbal*, trans by Khawaja Tariq
    Mahmood, (New Delhi: Star Publications, 2001).

Dr Ed Tronick & Dr Claudia M Gold, *The Power of Discord*
    (New York: Little Brown Spark, 2020).

Ibn al-Qayyim, *Al-Fawā'id*, trans. by Umm Al Qura, Bayan Translation Services (Al Mansura: 2004).

Ibn Sīnā, *Al-Urjūzah Fī Al-Ṭibb: Avicenna's Poem on Medicine*, ed and trans by Haven C. Krueger (Springer, 1963).

Mohammad Akram Nadwi, *Al-Muḥaddithāt: The Women Scholars in Islam* (Oxford: Interface, 2007).

Rokeya Sakhawat Hossain, *Woman's Downfall*, trans by Mohammad A. Quayum, *Transnational Literature*, Vol 4, no 1, November 2011.

Rokeya Sakhawat Hossain, *The Essential Rokeya: The Essential Works of Rokeya Sakhawat Hossain*, Trans by Mohammad A Quayum, (Boston: Brill, 2013).

The Majestic Qur'an: A Plain English Translation, trans by Musharraf Hussain (Nottingham: Invitation Publishing, 2019).

The Qur'an: English Translation and Parallel Arabic, trans by M. A. S. Abdel Haleem (Oxford: Oxford World Classics, 2010).